YOUR FOUR-POINT PL

Ursula Markham is a practising ...
with all aspects of stress control. S...
inars for companies on Stress Management and also ...
regular training courses in Time and Crisis Management,
Presentations, Public Speaking, Assertiveness Training
and Accelerated Learning Techniques. She lectures frequently in the UK and has also appeared on both radio
and television.

Your
FOUR-POINT PLAN
for Life

URSULA MARKHAM

E L E M E N T

Rockport, Massachusetts • Shaftesbury, Dorset

© Ursula Markham 1991

Published in Great Britain in 1991 by
Element Books Limited
Longmead, Shaftesbury, Dorset

Published in the USA in 1991 by
Element Inc
42 Broadway, Rockport, MA 01966

Designed by Roger Lightfoot
Cover illustration by Lesley Craig
Cover design by Max Fairbrother
Typeset by Input Typesetting Ltd
Printed and bound in Great Britain by
Billings Ltd, Hylton Road, Worcester

British Library Cataloguing in Publication Data
Markham, Ursula
Your four-point plan for life.
1. Self-realisation
I. Title
158.1

ISBN 1–85230–212–7

Contents

To Philip and David
with my love

All are but parts of one, stupendous whole,
Whose body Nature is, and God the soul.

Alexander Pope, 1688–1744

Introduction

If you try to make a cake without flour you are unlikely to be happy with the result. If you put some tender young plants in your garden and then fail to water them, they will be unlikely to thrive. If you buy yourself a shiny new car and then forget to check that there is petrol in the tank it will not run for long.

In each of the above examples, the lack of one essential ingredient would bring about failure to function properly. And yet we often expect that most precious of gifts – our life – to keep running smoothly even when we fail to ensure that all those essential ingredients are provided.

Naturally we are all different – and what a good thing we are, or the world would be a very boring place. It is because we are so different from each other that the way we all wish to live varies too. But, whatever our individual choices, to get the most out of living we need a balanced combination of all the essential ingredients. We need to have harmony between the four main aspects of ourselves – our physical, emotional, mental and spiritual selves.

Of course, it may be possible to create something vaguely edible even if one leaves the flour out of the mixture – but it will not be a cake. Some of your plants may not die, even if you do not water them – but they certainly will not thrive. If you remove the handbrake, your car may run downhill even without petrol in the tank – but that is not motoring. And it may be possible for you to exist without trying to achieve balance and harmony between the four aspects of yourself – but merely existing cannot compare with living life to the full.

The object of this book is to help you identify the points you have reached in your own development within each of the aspects mentioned, as well as identifying what you would like to aim for and how you can work towards achieving those aims by simple self-help methods.

Although the book is divided into four separate sections, each dealing with a different aspect of life – physical, emotional, mental and spiritual – it will become apparent as we go along that these four are so strongly interlinked that each will only function satisfactorily when combined with elements of the other three.

If you want to learn to make a cake you follow the recipe in a cookery book. If you want your garden to blaze with colour all summer long you consult a gardening book. If you would like to know how to look after your car you study a manual on motoring. Hopefully, by the time you have read this book, you will have found a way to live your life as you truly wish.

PART I

The Physical Self

1

The Body and its Needs

THE HOLISTIC APPROACH

It is so easy to think that we can keep our bodies fit and healthy simply by taking care of their physical needs. But that is far from the case. Of course, those physical needs must be looked after – but there is much more to it than that. As you will see, our emotions, our thought processes (both conscious and unconscious) and our self-awareness all play a large part in governing our physical health.

Just imagine what your reaction would be if you were given a brand new washing machine and told that it had to last you for seventy years or more. You would laugh, knowing that the impossible was being demanded. And you would be right. Oh, you might be careful to plumb that machine in correctly, to use only the right powder in the right quantity, never to overload it and to have it serviced regularly. But you would still not be surprised if it ended its useful life after ten years or so of daily use.

Isn't it strange that most of us do not pay the same careful attention to our body? We put in the wrong substances, we overload it and mistreat it and yet we still expect it to work efficiently and well, day in and day out, for the whole of our life. And then we are surprised and upset when it fails to do so.

If it is to function as well as it possibly can, the body has several basic needs – nutrition, exercise, relaxation, sleep and so on – but, because of the hectic pace of twentieth century life, not enough attention is paid to ensuring that these needs are met. In the General Household Survey, a national survey conducted in 1988, 70 per cent of the people questioned said that they hardly ever felt really well. These were not people with chronic or serious illnesses and yet they claimed that on most days they had some sort of ache or pain or just a feeling of being 'run down' or 'drained'.

It is easy to blame the pressure of daily life and the stress it causes for the fact that we do not feel as well as we should like – and, indeed, in many cases an excess of stress and tension may be the cause. But first let us examine the facts and then ensure that we are looking after our physical selves as well as possible. Once you have assured yourself that you are doing your best in this respect, you can go on to look at other possible causes, if you still feel generally unfit or without a zest for life.

EATING AND NUTRITION

There are many reasons why we eat – and it is certainly not simply to satisfy the pangs of hunger. If that were so, no one would ever eat or drink to excess. We have only to look at the animal kingdom; a creature in the wild will never overeat and, even if it has had to put effort into the hunting and killing of its prey, it will stop eating when it has had enough and walk away from the food. It is true to say that the only overweight animals are those cared for by humans who take more notice of the time on the clock than of natural feelings of hunger.

The western diet has changed dramatically over the past few decades. Many foods which were once thought of as 'exotic' are now readily available in every High Street. The advent of commercial and domestic freezing equipment means that what we eat is no longer limited by the time of year – although whether you consider the flavour of food which has been deep frozen for any length of time to be as good is another matter. More and more sprays and chemicals have been used on the food we eat and the land on which it is grown and ingenious methods of preserving the appearance of freshness have been devised. Add to this the fact that many people no longer have the time to bake their own bread and cakes or grow their own vegetables and you will see how the situation has changed even in the years since the end of the war. The 'take-away' industry has grown suddenly and dramatically, as has the consumption of vast quantities of junk foods – you only have to look at all those supermarket trolleys piled high with packets of crisps and cans of fizzy drink.

Now it is not my intention here to criticise any particular type of food or the individual who wishes to consume it. And it is true to say that, provided you do not suffer from any particular allergy or illness, a certain amount of food commonly considered to be 'bad' for you won't do you any harm at all. But the very fact that you are reading this book makes it probable that you wish to do the best for your health and that of your family; so what I would like to look at here is what is the best and healthiest nutritional intake for your body. And your body has certain needs, needs which are met when you have enough of the various vitamins, minerals and trace elements so essential to optimum health.

I do not wish to enter into the rights and wrongs of meat consumption versus vegetarianism or alcohol consumption versus abstention. That is a matter for personal belief and conscience alone. All I am trying to show is that it is possible to improve your general health and your sense of well-being by paying greater attention to what you put into your mouth and body.

It isn't easy for any of us today to be sure that we are getting all the vitamins that we need. The writing on a carton of orange juice may tell you that it contains a certain amount of vitamin C – but did you know that the vitamin C content starts to decrease from the moment the carton is opened? If you are drinking from it two or three days later, even if it has been refrigerated, the vitamin C has probably disappeared altogether.

If you are unsure about the adequacy of your daily diet, look at the list of symptoms below. If any of them apply to you, it is possible that you are deficient in the vitamin, mineral or trace element indicated. The second list tells you which foods naturally contain those items – but remember, if you really cannot bring yourself to eat a particular range of foods, it is always possible to take the lacking vitamin in tablet form.

Symptoms of deficiency	Vitamin, mineral or trace elements
Anaemia	Vitamin B12, Folic acid, Iron
Appetite poor	Vitamin B12, Phosphorus, Sodium
Bleeding prolonged	Vitamin K
Body tissue poor	Sulphur
Bone deformity	Vitamin D
Bones brittle or soft	Calcium
Bronchial problems	Vitamin A
Calcium deficiency	Vitamin D, Calcium
Catarrh	Vitamin A
Constipation	PABA, Iron
Dandruff	Vitamin F
Depression	Vitamin B1, PABA
Digestion poor	Chlorine
Energy loss	Copper, Iodine, Iron
Fatigue	Vitamin B12, Biotin, PABA
Growth retarded	Zinc
Hair and nail problems	Vitamin F
Hair, teeth loss	Chlorine
Headaches	Niacin
Heart/respiratory problems	Potassium
Incomplete pregnancies	Vitamin E
Insomnia	Vitamin B6, Niacin
Intestinal disorders	Niacin
Irritability	Vitamin B6, PABA
Joints painful	Vitamin C, Calcium
Low resistance to infection	Vitamins A, C
Mouth/tongue sores	Vitamins B2, C
Muscle cramp	Vitamin B6
Muscles weak	Sodium
Muscular disorders	Vitamin E

Symptoms of deficiency	Vitamin, mineral or trace elements
Nausea	Sodium
Nervous disorders	Vitamins B1, B2, E, Niacin, Magnesium
Night blindness	Vitamin A
Pernicious anaemia	Cobalt
Premature ageing	Vitamin E, Choline, Inositol
Rashes, spots	Vitamin B6, Niacin, Copper
Skin and hair problems	Vitamins B1, B2, B3, B12, Biotin, Iodine
Stamina poor	Vitamin B2
Sterility in men	Vitamin E
Thyroid enlarged	Iodine
Tooth decay	Vitamins C, D, Calcium
Trembling, shaking	Magnesium
Ulcers	Vitamin B1
Varicose veins	Vitamin F
Vision poor	Vitamin B2
Weight loss	Phosphorous

The list you have just looked at is designed to help you identify any deficiency you may have. It is in no way intended to replace any treatment you may be having from a doctor, consultant or practitioner. Should you experience any of the symptoms over a prolonged period of time, it is always advisable to have a check-up to ensure that you do not have a condition which requires professional help. If, like many people, you simply feel that you are 'a bit run down' or not as full of zest for life as you would wish, perhaps you could try ensuring that your diet contains all the nutrients essential for true well-being.

Suppose you have checked the list and decided which elements appear to be lacking in your daily diet, where are you to look for them? Ask anyone about vitamin C and they will be able to tell you that it is found in oranges – but would they also know that it is in melons and tomatoes? The table below will help you to identify the source of those elements (but do remember that we are talking about natural, as opposed to processed, foods).

Element	Found in:
Vitamin A	Green vegetables, liver, kidney, milk, cream, cheese
Vitamin B1	Green vegetables, milk, eggs, meat, liver, yeast, wheat ge.m
Vitamin B2	Green vegetables, peanuts, milk, eggs, meat, poultry, yeast, wheat germ
Vitamin B3	Brown rice, bran, liver, yeast, eggs, whole grain products
Vitamin B6	Milk, egg yolk, fish, yeast, wheat germ, melon, cabbage
Vitamin B12	Eggs, liver, meat, yeast, spinach, lettuce
Vitamin C	Citrus fruit, melon, tomatoes, raw vegetables, berries
Vitamin D	Milk, butter, fish, eggs, green vegetables
Vitamin E	Green vegetables, egg yolks, milk, seed germ oils
Vitamin F	Soya, corn oil
Vitamin K	Green leafy vegetables, soya beans, tomatoes, liver, vegetable oil
Biotin	Vegetables, nuts, liver, kidney
Choline	Egg yolk, dried yeast, liver, kidney
Folic Acid	Leafy green vegetables, brewer's yeast, liver
PABA (Para-aminobenzoic acid)	Liver, yeast, wheat germ, molasses
Inositol	Eggs, meat, liver, kidney, whole grain products
Niacin	Milk, liver, kidney, yeast, whole grain products
Cobalt	Milk, liver, kidney
Copper	Green leafy vegetables, liver, whole grain
Iodine	Plant and animal seafoods
Iron	Leafy green vegetables, liver, dried apricots, walnuts

Element	Found in:
Zinc	Brewer's yeast, wheat bran, wheat germ
Calcium	Milk, dairy products, bone meal
Chlorine	Sea salt
Magnesium	Green vegetables, apples, almonds, corn, soya beans
Phosphorous	Eggs, fish, poultry, meat, whole grain, nuts
Potassium	Leafy green vegetables, oranges, whole grain, potato skins
Sodium	Seafoods, sea salt, kelp, meat, beets
Sulphur	Eggs, fish, nuts, meat, cabbage, Brussels sprouts

The emotional approach to eating

There are many reasons why we eat – and a number of them have nothing whatsoever to do with hunger or even a liking for a particular type of food. Ask yourself whether any of the following could be your motivation for eating:

- I'm bored;
- It's one o'clock (or six, or ten or whatever time you usually have a meal);
- I enjoy the sensation of eating;
- I feel miserable;
- We're going to a restaurant for dinner so I want to have something special;
- I feel deprived if I can't have the same as everyone else;
- I can't tell the difference between being hungry and wanting food;
- I'm worried/nervous/anxious.

Of course, just as there are people who turn to the cake-tin when they are anxious, there are others who find themselves unable to eat at all. They may seek consolation in alcohol or in black coffee and cigarettes.

The solution to the problem is the same in both cases. By learning to understand the effect of their emotional state upon their eating habits, the people concerned will become more aware of what they are – or are not – taking into their bodies. This is why the balance between the different parts of the human self is so very important and why we should all seek to achieve that balance if we possibly can.

Annette was a typical worry-eater. If her husband was very late home from work, if water began to drip through the ceiling or the gas bill was far larger than usual – Annette's immediate reaction was to rush to the bread bin or the biscuit jar.

Then one day she had a real reason to worry. Someone came to tell her that her twelve-year-old son Paul had been knocked down by a car on the way home from a friend's house and taken to the local hospital. Fortunately the boy had not been too badly hurt but he did require minor surgery in addition to the treatment of several cuts and bruises. For various reasons, including the fact that he had recently eaten, it was not thought wise to operate until about 10pm that night.

Annette spent the intervening time with her son who had been made as comfortable as possible and she told him that she would stay with him until he went for the operation and would then go home but would return first thing in the morning. The boy was taken into the operating theatre just before ten and Annette went home, the surgeon having promised to telephone her as soon as it was all over.

Once home – and although she had eaten nothing for several hours – Annette found that she could not face the thought of a meal, even though her husband offered to prepare one for her. She just sat on the stairs eating biscuit after biscuit until, just before midnight, the telephone rang and she heard the voice of the surgeon telling her that the operation was over, that it had been a complete success and that Paul was likely to make a rapid recovery. It was after that call that Annette realised that she had steadily munched her way through two and a half packets of biscuits. She had not enjoyed them –

indeed, she had not even tasted them. She had simply eaten one after another to try and stem the feelings of anxiety within her.

Once a worry-eater – usually a woman – learns to become more aware of herself and her emotions in the way shown in Part II, she will be more able to control her reactions to stress and anxiety and less likely to turn to food for comfort.

Know what you eat

Eating should be a pleasure and not merely a means of fuelling the body. But this is rarely the case. So many of us are accustomed to eating in front of the television, or at a desk or even rushing about in the morning clutching a briefcase in one hand and a piece of toast in the other. Not only do we not enjoy what we eat; in many instances we do not even notice what it tastes like.

Try this simple exercise which will help you to increase your awareness of what you are eating:

1. Select a plain food which you know you enjoy – perhaps an apple, a piece of cheese or a slice of bread. Put it on a plate and find a quiet place to sit where you will not be disturbed by other people, by the radio or by the telephone.
2. Allow yourself to relax. Let the tension flow out of your body. Take a few deep breaths.
3. Look at the food on your plate. Think about its colour, its shape and its size.
4. Before you even think of tasting it, pick it up, being aware of how it feels and how it smells.
5. Take a small bite and think about the taste. Is it hot or cold; sweet, sharp or bitter? Chew it slowly, allowing the taste to fill your senses. Chew it many times before you swallow it.
6. Pause for a few moments before repeating the process to ensure that you are as relaxed as possible.

Now naturally you are not going to eat like that all the time – it would be foolish and impractical. But we would all do well to learn to eat more slowly and to savour the taste of what we are eating. Our bodies would be able to make far better use of the nutrients in the food and we would get more pleasure from the whole process. In addition, it would make us far less likely to eat for the wrong reasons.

Here are a few suggestions which you may find helpful:

* It is better to have several small meals in a day than a few heavy ones. You may not want to get up and run a race immediately after eating but you should not eat so much that you find it difficult to climb a flight of stairs. A heavy meal is far more likely to make you want to sleep – just think of Christmas!

* Personal preference naturally varies but more benefit is to be gained by having a reasonable breakfast and lunch and a smaller evening meal (even though most of us are used to doing it the other way around). If you also have snacks between the meals your metabolism is likely to work far more efficiently. However, a 'snack' does not have to mean crisps, biscuits or chocolate; there are plenty of nutritious things such as nuts, raisins or fruit.

* Enjoy what you eat. If you don't enjoy it, what is the point of eating it? Find something else.

* Forget all those things your mother told you! Finishing every last morsel on your plate won't make your hair curl or do anything to help the starving children in India. You may decide that you wish to eat less in future and send the money you save to a worthy cause – but it's far too late to do anything now with that extra roast potato or the last spoonful of pudding. If you have had enough, stop eating. Most of us in the western world are fortunate in that we know where the next meal is coming from. There is no need for us to act like hedge-hogs, eating all that we can to fill ourselves up for the coming months.

* Eating never fixed a broken heart! Comfort eating usually involves the consumption of sweets, cakes and so on. After all, there's nothing particularly comforting

about a cold stick of celery, is there? In many cases, mummy used to give you a sweet to 'make it better' or because you had been 'good'. You may even have been deprived of your favourite goodies as a punishment when you were naughty. All this is stored in the sub-conscious memory and the habit continues when we grow up. But, although that sweet may have made you forget a grazed knee when you were four years old, I have never heard of a chocolate (or even a whole box of them) bringing back a lost love, changing the grade on an examination paper or reversing an unwelcome redundancy.

* A little habit is a mindless thing. Next time you go to the cinema, just take a look at the blank faces of most of the audience as they stare at the screen while simultaneously chomping their way through a ridiculous amount of sweets, hot-dogs or popcorn. They are not really enjoying what they are eating; they are not even noticing what they are eating; they are certainly not satisfying feelings of hunger. It is just that going to the cinema has become inexorably linked with the purchase and consumption of such foods. The management of the cinema will even make sure there is an interval during the performance so that the sale of ice-cream, nuts and drinks can take place. One can hardly blame them but you can be sure that they are not thinking that those poor people in the audience must be feeling hungry – they simply want to increase their profits. I am not being a killjoy. If you enjoy a bag of popcorn when you go to the cinema, then by all means have it. But be sure that you do enjoy it. Taste it, savour it – don't simply chew and swallow, chew and swallow like a robot, hardly even knowing what you are eating.

Stimulants/addiction

What do we usually do in times of stress, or if we feel that we need cheering up? We have a cup of tea or coffee (or even something stronger). We have grown accustomed to using tea and coffee as a pick-me-up when we are feeling low. But both of these contain caffeine and other chemical stimulants which are quickly absorbed into the bloodstream. If you feel that you want a cup of tea, or coffee because you enjoy the taste for its own sake, then go ahead and have one. But, for the sake of your own well-being, it would be best to try and reduce the number that you have in the course of the day. You might try drinking mineral water or fruit juice or one of the many varieties of herbal teas with their delicate and delicious flavours. Remember, however, that because those stimulants are addictive, if your consumption has been particularly high you are likely to suffer withdrawal symptoms (headaches, lethargy and so on) if you try and cut the stimulants out completely in one fell swoop. Such symptoms are far less likely to trouble you if you gradually reduce your intake until you are able to go without the substances altogether.

Alcohol

For most people alcohol does not present too great a problem provided it is taken in moderation. But only drink it if you enjoy the taste and sensation. If you take it to make yourself numb, in order to forget or to help you sleep, you are only using it to mask the symptoms of a distressing situation which will still be there tomorrow. And anyone who has ever seen the devastating effects of alcohol addiction on the alcoholic, his or her friends and family will understand only too well the dramatic and destructive influence it can have on the lives of all concerned.

Tobacco

Tobacco is not a food or drink but it is something which is taken into the body through the mouth (and nose). And the harm it can do may be greater than anyone realises. It is not only cancer which has to be taken into consideration but such life-threatening problems as emphysema, bronchitis, hardening of the arteries and heart disease. I know we have all heard of cases where someone has smoked sixty cigarettes a day and still lived to a ripe old age – but is it really worth taking the chance?

If you have children and you smoke, you have even more to worry about. It is not simply a matter of the harm done by passive smoking but it is an accepted fact that the children of smokers are far more likely to adopt the habit themselves. Suppose you actually managed to escape all the harmful effects of tobacco but your child took up smoking because you smoked and he or she went on to develop one of those dreadful (and often fatal) illnesses. Would you ever forgive yourself?

Picture the surface of a busy road on a very hot day in summer. You will have seen how that road surface can become soft and sticky in extreme heat. But, once the temperature has cooled down, the surface of the road is hard again and tough enough for one lorry after another to drive along. That road is coated with tar – the same substance found, to a greater or lesser degree, in cigarettes. It may be soft and warm as you inhale it but once it is inside your body it becomes as hard and tough as the surface of that road.

Drugs

I am not qualified to write in detail about such substances as LSD, cocaine and heroin but I am sure you will agree that there is no way that they can be part of a healthy and balanced lifestyle. This is not only because of the harmful effects they can have on the physical self but also because the need for them indicates a severe deficiency in the emotional self – a deficiency which needs to be helped and treated rather than disguised.

There are, however, many people who are addicted to tranquillisers of one sort or another. While I have great sympathy for the doctors of twenty years or more ago who did not realise the addictive effect of such tablets when they began to prescribe them, I do not feel equal sympathy for those doctors (fortunately their number is growing less) who still hand out similar prescriptions to their patients and then fail to monitor their progress or to help them give up the medication as soon as possible.

If you are unfortunate enough to be suffering from tranquilliser addiction, there are a few very important points to remember:

* *Never* try to stop taking them all at once. It is vitally important that you cut down gradually – preferably with help, whether from your doctor or a practitioner of alternative medicine.
* There are several non-addictive herbal and non-chemical remedies which can help you while you are withdrawing from your prescribed tranqillisers. These will not have the same 'blanket' effect, but they will make it easier to cut your dose down.
* Because tranquillisers simply mask symptoms rather than provide a cure, you may need to seek help to deal with the problem which caused you to need the tablets in the first place. Don't be afraid to ask for such help – a problem is a problem, whether it is a broken leg or an emotional upset. (In the next chapter you will find information about some of the therapies which may be helpful to you.)

ACTIVITY AND EXERCISE

How our lives have changed in the course of just a few decades. Not so many years ago parents would have thought nothing of their children walking two or three miles to school in the morning and back again in the afternoon. Now, partly because of fears for their safety and partly because of increased affluence, many children are either taken to school by car or they travel by 'bus or train. At one time those same children, on getting home in the afternoon, would have gone out to play – climbing trees, going fishing, playing football, running races. Now they are more likely to spend their time sitting in front of the television, watching videos or staring at a computer screen.

Their parents' lives have changed too. Modern technology has seen to that, giving them a machine to make their early morning tea and even an electronic handset to save them having to get out of their chairs in the evening to change the television channel. There is now a social status attached to non-manual jobs, to being a two-car family and so on. It looks as if the day may not be so far away when we can all do our shopping, banking and working from our homes. I am neither condoning nor criticising all these changes but it is vital that we do something to counteract this decrease in activity.

The last few years have seen the age of the fitness fanatics – those who rush headlong to join in the latest craze whether it is jogging, aerobics or weight training. This is fine if you actually *enjoy* such activities but all too often enthusiasm quickly wanes. The problem arises because there is nothing in our day-to-day life to provide us with sufficient exercise.

Suppose you are one of those people who really hates any form of organised exercise, what can you do? Perhaps you could go for a walk each day (with or without a dog); you could go swimming or ride a bicycle – it doesn't really matter what you do as long as you do it regularly.

Why exercise?

Help your heart: The heart is a muscular pump and, just like the muscles in your arms and legs, it needs regular exercise. Hippocrates (the father of modern medicine) said that anything which is used develops while anything which is not used simply wastes away. Regular (as opposed to sudden or extreme) exercise improves the coronary circulation. This not only helps to prevent heart attacks but is also used to aid the recovery of those who have already suffered them.

In the early 1960s the Mayo Clinic in Minnesota researched exercise therapy as part of the treatment for patients suffering from angina. Eight patients were studied in detail and were given supervised exercise therapy. After twelve months five of these patients were free of all symptoms of angina while the other three found that their spasms were less frequent and less severe.

Regular and steady exercise reduces the blood pressure; therefore the heart doesn't have to work so hard. So, however full, busy or stressed your life may be, making time for exercise can be beneficial in counteracting the tension caused.

Exercise also reduces the body's cholesterol level. Although cholesterol has come to be regarded as some sort of evil, a certain amount is actually essential for some aspects of physical health such as repairing lining membranes and the manufacture of sex hormones. As with many things, it is the *excess* which is harmful; regular exercise can help to reduce this excess and may allow the alterations in eating habits to be a little less drastic. (I am not, however, suggesting that if you exercise it will be possible to live on a diet of eggs, butter and cream – moderation in all things!)

Maintain or improve condition of muscles, bones and ligaments: Have you ever had to spend any length of time flat on your back in bed – perhaps due to illness or an accident? If you have, you will know how weak your muscles were when first you tried to get up and walk again. That may be a drastic example but it is as well to remember that the less we use our muscles the less efficient they will be. Taken to extremes, muscles will waste, joints will stiffen and bones will fracture more easily.

Physiotherapists in the United States have begun taking a form of mobile weight-training apparatus to old age homes. There they have been working with individual patients who, for one reason or another, spend most of their lives sitting down – some of them in wheelchairs, unable to walk at all. Starting very gradually, they have built up an exercise routine for each patient designed to suit their particular needs and they have found that the results have been quite dramatic. Not only have the elderly people enjoyed the challenge and the attention but their physical strength has improved considerably. Indeed, one old lady of 94 was interviewed on television and she proudly told the presenter 'I can now walk faster than my daughter – and she's only 72!'

Lose weight or inches: Exercise alone is unlikely to bring about a great weight loss – in fact you would have to run about two miles to use up 200 calories. But, because it tones up the muscles and firms the body, you may well lose inches. In addition, exercise does help to control the appetite so it may help you to reduce your intake – thus bringing about a weight loss in an indirect way.

Improve your mood and counteract stress: Ask anyone who exercises regularly and they will tell you that they always feel exhilarated at the end of a session – even if they had begun by feeling that they were not in the mood for exercise and had almost forced themselves to continue. Physical fitness also provides considerable protection against stress and the illnesses it can cause. So, however busy your life, perhaps you could try and fit some regular exercise into your day. Let it be something which is in complete contrast to the way you normally spend your time. One word of warning though: if you are someone whose daily life involves a strong competitive element, you would do well to avoid too much in the way of competitive sport (squash, tennis and so on) as your form of exercise as these will only tend to maintain an already high level of stress.

Increase your mental ability: Research has shown that, all other things being equal, the person who exercises regularly performs better in tests requiring mental agility. So, in addition to getting fitter, you are likely to find that you are better at making decisions, doing your job, passing exams – or simply completing the crossword.

What sort of exercise?

Frankly, provided you follow a few basic rules (see below), it really doesn't matter. You may want to join a club and work out three times a week or you may simply decide to walk to work instead of going by car or 'bus. If you can't make up your mind what is best for you, ask yourself these questions:

– Do I want to follow a set exercise programme or would I prefer to change my life-style so that I become more active?
– Would I rather exercise alone, with a friend or in a group?
– Am I more likely to continue exercising if I join a class where there is a certain amount of discipline?
– Do I want to vary my exercise and enjoy a combination of swimming, running and so on?
– Would I prefer simply to fit a sequence of exercises into my daily routine?

I mentioned that there are a few basic rules which you should bear in mind if your exercising is not to do you more harm than good. Most of them are common sense but you would be surprised how, in our eagerness to succeed, we often forget them.

1. If you have not exercised for some time, if you are generally unfit or if you know you have a particular medical condition, it is essential to consult your doctor before beginning a regular exercise routine.
2. Start slowly. When the fitness craze first took hold, both in Britain and in the United States, some people threw themselves into an orgy of aerobics, weight training or jogging with the result that quite a large number of them suffered injuries of one sort or another. If it is some time since you last exercised on a regular basis, spend a few weeks following a gentle stretching and warming-up routine. Even when you are fitter, it is a good idea to start each session with these, just as athletes and ballet dancers do throughout their careers.

3. Don't push too hard. Build your own routine up gradually. An exercise session shouldn't cause any agony or leave you feeling exhausted. If you find that you cannot hold a normal conversation after exercising, then you are overdoing it.
4. If you feel any pain or strain – stop! This applies whether you are just starting on a simple routine or whether you have already built up to one which is more strenuous.
5. Little and often is the way to achieve maximum benefit. You will not do a great deal of good if you do nothing from Monday to Saturday and then run five miles on Sunday.
6. Enjoy it. There is no point at all in starting to do something you hate or which you find boring because you will never stick to it.
7. For real benefit, allow your exercise to help you on more than simply a physical level. Become aware of your body, of your breathing pattern and of the link between feelings of physical and mental well-being.
8. Exercise for *yourself* rather than to impress or conform with anyone else. Although competitive sports are fine, the type of exercise we are talking about here should not involve competition, particularly if you are the type of person who usually feels that winning is important. If you are to achieve harmony of mind and body, allow yourself to feel joy in your own achievement without always having to feel that it must be better than someone else's.

Activity value

Listed below are many of the most popular forms of exercise and their activity values on a scale of 1 to 10. If your chosen exercise has a value of five or more, then practising it for twenty minutes, three times a week, should be sufficient to maintain a level of basic fitness. However, if the score is less than five, you will need to increase the amount of time spent or the number of times a week you practise it.

(In setting out this table, the assumption is made that you are fit enough to practise your chosen form of exercise without doing yourself any harm. The figures do not take into account the stress which may be caused by the competitive element involved; they relate simply to the physical benefits.)

Exercise	Activity value
Archery	3.50
Badminton	4.75
Basketball	6.95
Billiards/snooker	2.00
Cricket	4.50
Cycling	8.00
Fencing	8.50
Fishing	2.00
Football	8.25
Golf	2.75
Gymnastics	7.50
Horse riding	4.00
Ice skating	7.50
Judo	10.00
Roller skating	7.50
Rowing	9.50
Skipping	8.50
Squash	9.50
Swimming	9.50
Table tennis	3.00
Tennis	5.75
Ten-pin bowling	3.00
Water skiing	5.25
Walking/running:	
1 km. in 15 mins.	2.75
1 km. in 7.5 mins.	6.50
1 km. in 5 mins.	9.50

SLEEP

Sleep is a natural healer of mind and body and yet many of the most common problems experienced relate to difficulties concerned with sleep. Either the individual

cannot get to sleep in the first place or he wakes frequently during the night. Sometimes he is beset by dis-
turbing dreams or sensations while asleep. More and
more people are turning to tablets to help them improve
the quality of their sleep but, as you will see, there are
simpler and more natural methods which are, at the
same time, far more effective.

Common sleep problems

* Difficulty in getting to sleep. This doesn't matter on the
odd occasion; it is only a problem if it occurs regularly. It
might be an idea to consider whether you have 'programmed yourself' to be an insomniac by telling yourself
that you are one of those people who 'never finds it easy
to fall asleep'.
* You go to sleep quickly enough but find that you wake
frequently during the night. Why do you think this is?
Are you worried about something? Even if you have
problems, there is very little you can do about them in
the middle of the night. You may find it helpful to keep
a pad and pen by the bed and write down any anxiety
which might come into your head. Once it's down in
black and white, you know you can't forget it so you
can put it out of your mind until the next day. And
remember, it is not necessary to be asleep in order to
refresh your mind and body; you simply need to be
mentally and physically relaxed – and there are techniques you can learn to help you achieve this.
* You don't feel that you sleep for long enough. What
is 'long enough'? There is no chart telling us just how
many hours we should be sleeping; indeed it varies
greatly from person to person. If you know that you feel
fit and well during the course of the day, then you are
getting sufficient sleep for your own needs.
* You wake in the morning feeling 'sluggish' and find it
difficult to get out of bed. Ignore how you feel when
you first wake and take note instead of how you feel
after you have been up for about ten minutes – many
people find those first waking moments difficult to cope

with. And remember that some of us are 'larks' who find it easy to be bright and efficient early in the morning but need to go to bed relatively early at night. Others are 'owls' for whom the reverse is true.

Finding the cause of the problem

* Check the vitamin/mineral list (page 9), as a deficiency in one of these can cause sleep problems.
* Ask yourself whether you are going through an emotionally upsetting period in your life. It is natural to find sleeping difficult if you have just suffered a bereavement or you are experiencing difficulties in a close relationship. Do what you can to deal with the problem during the day and be aware that sleeping difficulties are temporary and will pass with time.
* Are you in the habit of eating or drinking immediately before going to bed?
* Is there something different about your immediate environment which may be causing you to feel unsettled? It may take a little time to adjust to anything, from strange surroundings to a new mattress.
* Are you suffering from an excess of stress in your life? If so, you need a winding-down time just before going to bed.

Self-help methods to help sleep

Even if none of the above causes apply in your case, try one or more of the following:
* Do something relaxing last thing before going to bed. You might decide to watch television, listen to music or read a book – but make sure that you enjoy it and that it has nothing to do with your work.
* Ensure that you have some physical exercise during the day – although not just before going to bed or your heart/pulse rate will increase and you will find sleeping even more difficult.

* Avoid food and drink (particularly tea and coffee) last thing at night as these can act as a stimulant.
* Make sure you have plenty of fresh air in the bedroom. Keeping a window open is helpful even when the weather is cold (provided you are warm in bed). Of course you should close it should conditions be foggy. Avoid smoking (your own or anyone else's) in the bedroom – just think of all that stale smoke you will be inhaling during the night.
* Establishing a pre-sleep routine is a good idea. It helps to create a pattern in the subconscious mind so that, as you go about your routine actions, the mind automatically prepares itself for sleep.
* If you have a bath just before bedtime, see that it is neither too hot nor too cold.
* Avoid that alcoholic 'nightcap'. It might help you to doze off but you will probably find that you wake during the night and cannot get back to sleep again.
* If you have a warm drink, try milk, cocoa or a herbal drink such as camomile tea.
* Your bedding should be enough to keep you warm but not too heavy. The same goes for nightclothes – avoid anything constricting.
* Try using one of the audio cassettes specially designed to help overcome insomnia (details in information section at end of book).
* Practise a relaxation exercise. There are many different ones but this will work as well as any other:

Close your eyes and lie in a comfortable position. Now, starting with your feet and working upwards, tense and relax each set of muscles in turn, finishing with the muscles of the neck and head. Spend a few moments establishing a slow and regular breathing pattern. Really listen to the rhythm of your breathing. Now picture a beautiful scene in brilliant sunshine – you might choose to visualise somewhere you know or to create a perfect place in your imagination. As you look at the place you have chosen, daylight turns to dusk; the colours become muted and the shadows lengthen. Then night falls and, by the light of the moon, you can just make out shapes and outlines – the scene is still beautiful but in a calmer and less vibrant way. (It is important at each stage to take the time to study the effect of the different types of light upon your chosen image rather than to use your mind to *tell* you what is happening.)

RELAXATION

Breathing

Do you ever stop and think about the way you breathe? Not often, I suspect. Oh, you may notice that you get out of breath when you have been running or that you hold your breath when frightened. But I wonder how aware you are of your breathing pattern the rest of the time.

The way in which we breathe affects our physical, mental and emotional well-being. With every breath we *should* take in half a litre of oxygen, twenty per cent of which goes to the brain. If that oxygen to the brain should cease for just ten seconds the result is a coma; after three minutes there is irreversible brain damage. It has been found, however, that most people only use about half their breathing potential which means the brain is only receiving about half its quota of oxygen.

Think of the vicious circle of hyperventilation. When we get into a panic (often through stress, fear or anxiety), our breathing become rapid and shallow. We find ourselves less able to think clearly as the oxygen intake diminishes and our panic therefore becomes greater. If someone's natural breathing is already shallow, that person is much more likely to panic in the first place.

Next time you are with a group of people, look around you and see how many of them breathe through the mouth. And yet it is important to breathe through the nose as the air taken in is then warmed and moistened before entering the lungs.

The benefits of controlled breathing can be seen in so many cases. It can assist in diminishing the effects of an asthma attack and is an integral part of the childbirth process. It can help in cases of insomnia, high blood pressure, tension and heart conditions – to name but a few. Because breathing is something we do spontaneously, we very rarely think about it. If controlled breathing through your nose is not natural to you, it takes practice and concentration at first but it will soon become second nature – and you will feel better for it.

Here is a simple exercise you can do which will help you to become aware of how your breathing *should* feel. If you practise it for just ten minutes each day, you will soon begin to notice the difference:

Lie on a bed or on the floor. Make sure nothing is restricting you – take off shoes, belts and ties. Close your eyes and listen to your breathing, trying to regulate the rhythm and making sure that you breathe only through your nose. Awareness of your breathing is important – just as awareness is important in any area of living. Place one hand on your chest and the other just below the ribcage. You should be able to feel your ribcage expand and contract but there should be as little movement as possible in your chest. Visualise the air you breathe in as clean and white and the air you exhale as dark and black, which takes with it both the toxins of the body and the troubles of the mind. If any worrying thoughts enter your mind, don't try and *force* them out. Look at them, acknowledge them and then tell yourself you will deal with them later and let them go.

Physical relaxation

How often we hear one person tell another to 'relax' as if it were the easiest thing in the world to do? Not only is it difficult to let go of tension, but most people don't even realise when they are becoming tense. It is obvious enough if you happen to be going through a particularly traumatic time, but what about when you are doing all those ordinary things like reading, writing, driving or pursuing any so-called 'relaxing' activity? What about now? Stop and think about your body. Can you feel tension in your neck and shoulders? Is your jaw clenched tightly? Are you frowning? And yet all you are doing is reading a book.

The keyword here is *awareness*. It is important to understand what it feels like to be truly relaxed and to become aware of those times when we are not. If your upper muscles (head, shoulders, neck and jaw) are tense, then that tension is being transmitted to the rest of your body and thence to your mind. And a mind which is affected by stress or tension cannot think as clearly. In addition, when tension strikes, the creative and intuitive elements are seriously hampered and it is easy to become negative in outlook.

It also works the other way around. If you are suffering from mental or emotional stress, your body will be adversely affected. Now the person does not exist who is going to travel through life without experiencing the highs and lows – not to mention all those feelings in between – and indeed it would be a pretty boring life if that were the case. And I am not suggesting that learning to relax will change a single external circumstance; what it will change is the effect those external circumstances have on your mind and body.

True relaxation is something which can be learned by anyone – although, like anything worth having, it does take a little practice. If you will spend just ten or fifteen minutes a day practising a simple relaxation technique, you will begin to feel the benefit within a matter of days. There are several methods you can use and of course you must find the one which suits you best but, as a starting-point, here is a simple and effective one:

Lie on your bed or sit in a chair with a back which is high enough to support your neck and head. Close your eyes and ensure that your breathing is slow and rhythmic. Beginning with your feet, concentrate on each group of muscles in turn, imagining them growing heavier and heavier. Pay particular attention to the muscles in your neck, shoulders and jaw and those around your eyes. Now take your mind on a walk. Picture a beautiful scene – whatever kind of landscape pleases you the most –

and imagine that you are walking through that place. Look at everything around you; be aware of the weather; listen to any noises which you might hear. As you walk along the scene will change slightly and there will be more things for you to experience. Be conscious of the fact that this is a tranquil and a peaceful place and that it belongs to you. Stay in your special place for several minutes, enjoying the experience. Then when you feel ready, open your eyes.

Once you have become used to the exercise you will find that it helps you on many an occasion when you feel tension mounting within you. To start with, you might have to go through the whole exercise in order to relax again but, once you have been doing it for some time, you will find that all you need to do is to picture your own peaceful scene and, because the link is permanently there in your subconscious mind, you will immediately begin to feel more peaceful, both mentally and physically.

Learning to relax is not simply a pleasant thing to do. By freeing your mind and body of excess tension, you are also lessening your chances of suffering from such stress-induced illnesses as strokes or heart attacks as well as any number of less life-threatening (but nonetheless distressing) problems, such as insomnia, constant headaches, pre-menstrual tension and so on.

I hope I have shown that caring for your physical health involves mental, emotional and spiritual processes too. And by improving the condition of any one of these four vital aspects of yourself, you will actually be improving the other three and thereby the quality of the life you live.

2

Help and Self-help

VITAL LIVING

The dictionary gives two different definitions of the word
'living'. The first is simple – 'being alive'; the second is
'lively, having vitality'. It is up to you to choose the
definition by which you wish to live your life. You can
'be alive' as opposed to 'being dead'; or you can do your
best to live life to the full – putting in and getting out
as much as possible.

This is where true holism comes in. To live life to the
full involves awareness of the physical, emotional,
mental and spiritual self. And all the aspects are interde-
pendent. You have only to think how often we suffer
from aches and pains when we are miserable or
depressed. Conversely, learning to develop a positive
mental attitude can dramatically improve our physical
health. 'I never catch a cold' says A – and indeed he
doesn't. But B *knows* that he will catch everything going
– and so he does. Yet both of them must come into
contact with the same assortment of germs and viruses
in their daily lives. Even recovery from something as
basically physical as a broken leg will be more rapid
when the patient has a determined and optimistic outlook on life.

The negative outlook: Negativity creates a vicious circle all its own. Look at the diagram below and see how misery or depression can lead to physical symptoms – which in turn make you feel even more miserable.

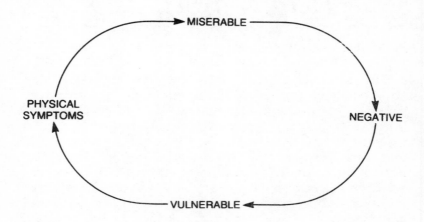

The positive outlook: However positive any individual may be, naturally he or she will encounter problems in different areas of life. But you will find that, for such a person, recovery will be speedier and more complete. After all, our positive friend has so much to look forward to that there is no time to be indisposed. And there are some wonderfully positive people among those who have permanent disabilities or terminal illnesses so it is not just a case of being one of the 'lucky' ones.

All this has nothing at all to do with money or financial status. Of course we all need a certain amount in order to exist – and it's rather nice to have a bit to spare. But, if you think money is the answer, you have only to read the newspapers to see how many of the more affluent members of society experience the trauma of divorce, drug or alcohol addiction or a suicide in the family.

So how does one go about becoming a more positive person? Well, you can start by trying to live each day to the full; cram in all the good things you can. Yes, I know you have chores and duties, many of them boring – you

have to go to work, make the supper, bath the children
. . . and so on. But there are so many things to gladden
the heart which take little time and no money. Simply
going for a walk can relax the mind and refresh the spirit
– and it will make you fitter too.

Holistic vitality boosters

1. *Live the natural way:* No, I am not suggesting that
you return to some sort of Tarzan and Jane existence,
simply that you try and reduce your dependence on
those mechanical things which sometimes seem to
threaten to take over our lives. Each of them has a value
and a part to play but *they* should serve *us*; we should
not be *their* slaves. Television is fine provided you are
selective in your viewing, but not if it is on all the time.
Many of the programmes do little to stimulate the mind
and sitting in a chair staring at a screen is not too good
for the body either. Think of how you could be spending
your time instead; you could go swimming, make model
aeroplanes or learn to yodel – it doesn't matter what you
do as long as it is fun!

Legs came before cars, mind and hands before videos
and computers. Try using them more often and you will
get more enjoyment out of life and be healthier too.

Spend as much time as possible in the open air. If you
have to spend the major part of the day in an office,
house or factory, can you open the windows? The Medical Research Council's Common Cold Research Unit
showed that it is not the person who gets caught in the
rain or sits in a draught who is likely to develop a cold
but the one who has to work in the air-conditioned,
centrally-heated, artificially-lit atmosphere found in many
modern office blocks. If you are someone who has to
spend much of your day in such conditions, it is even
more important that you try to absorb as much fresh air
as possible in your leisure time.

2. *Eat natural foods:* The human body was made to cope
with a diet of nuts, cereals, meat and raw vegetables,

not a mixture of cakes, pastries and potato crisps. The more you are able to stick to a diet of natural foods – fruit and vegetables (raw if possible), wholemeal products and so on – the healthier your body is likely to be. However, fanaticism is not the answer. Nothing terrible will befall if you eat a piece of pizza – only if you exist on a diet of nothing but pizza. One slice of chocolate gateau is not going to ruin your health – but several slices a day may well do so.

In recent years that word 'fibre' has loomed large in our lives. We all know how vital it is for good health. And yet many foods are now refined to such an extent that the natural fibre has been removed. And what do we do? On the one hand, we eat all those pre-packed and refined foods and, on the other, we sprinkle bran over everying from soup to yoghourt. It is much simpler, cheaper and healthier to try and eat a high-fibre diet in the first place. You will not only lose weight and have greater vitality, you will also find that you are able to think more clearly and are less likely to suffer from stress.

3. Listen to your body: Once again, it is a case of being *aware*. Aware of how you feel and what your body is telling you. Perhaps you always have your evening meal at seven o'clock – but, if you are hungry at six, that is when you should eat. And, if seven o'clock comes and you are aware that you do not feel hungry – don't eat. As I write, I can almost hear the protests of those with families to feed – 'It's the one time we can all sit down together' or 'I don't have time to cook several different meals each evening'. But no one has said that you cannot sit at the table and talk to your family, even if you choose not to eat. And there is no need to prepare separate meals – just save yours until later when you do feel hungry.

What about bedtime? Are you someone who *always* goes to bed at 11pm? If you are aware that you do not feel tired, try staying up a little later – it has to be better than lying there wondering why you can't get to sleep. But, if tonight you find yourself yawning at 9.30, why not have an early night? Of course there are times when this is not possible for practical reasons, but the more you are able to stay in tune with your body, the better you will feel.

Are your clothes comfortable? If your shoes pinch – take them off. And, as soon as time and money permits, buy a more comfortable pair. If your waistband is too tight, loosen it. You can decide later whether to let it out or try and lose some weight.

Do you feel happy? Then laugh. Are you weary? Have a rest and leave the washing up till later. Does a moving film make you tearful? Then cry – don't try and stifle your emotions for fear of looking 'silly'. Why should it be silly to feel deeply?

4. *Don't get your health out of a bottle:* There are, of course, certain medical conditions which make the taking of professionally prescribed drugs essential. But there are also thousands of people walking around in a semi-drugged state day after day because they are in the habit of taking tablets, whether prescribed or bought over the counter. We have all heard of the addiction caused by long-term taking of tranquillisers but did you realise that the effect of sleeping pills can last well into the following day and many antihistamines (commonly taken to relieve colds or allergies) can make you so drowsy that you should not drive for some hours after taking them?

Relying on tablets for the relief of pain without trying to discover its cause can be positively dangerous. Unless you have a specific allergy, there is no great harm in taking something to relieve an isolated headache. But pain is there for a reason; it is a warning signal, telling you that something is wrong and, as such, should not be ignored. A simple headache may be just that – perhaps as a result of tension or over-tiredness. A constantly recurring headache could indicate that your eyesight needs checking or even, in more drastic cases, that you have a brain tumour. Whatever the cause, any pain which is constant or which occurs frequently should be investigated.

Many of the more readily available forms of medication

treat the *symptom* and, of course, much short-term relief can be obtained in this way. Holism, however, involves treating the whole person so that, hopefully, the underlying condition which brings about the symptom can be dealt with.

SELF-HELP METHODS FOR HOLISTIC HEALING

Please remember that, should you suffer from a chronic or acute complaint, these methods are best used in conjunction with whatever form of treatment you are receiving – whether from orthodox medicine or a qualified complementary practitioner.

If you feel the need to take 'medicine', whether in liquid or tablet form, why not try one of the many herbal remedies now available? These are easy to obtain from health shops or through specialised catalogues and have the advantage of being free from chemicals and therefore non-addictive. Also effective are the Bach Flower Remedies although these are sometimes a little harder to find. (Please see bibliography for details of informative books on these subjects.)

There are many other self-help methods available, some of which will be dealt with later in other sections of this book. These include the use of relaxation (see page 137) for insomnia, nervous tension, high blood pressure and other stress-related conditions. Visualisation (see page 146), involving positive use of the imagination, can bring about dramatic results in cases ranging from the comparatively trivial to the life-threatening.

Finding a therapist to help you

Many complementary therapies exist which are concerned with holistic healing. The major ones are detailed here but, should you decide that you wish to consult such a therapist, there are a few points to remember:

1. Choosing your therapist: Make sure the therapist you

consult is properly qualified – don't be afraid to ask. It is not a good idea simply to rely on advertisements in the local paper but far better to go to someone who has been recommended to you by a friend who has been successfully treated. Or you can write to one of the reputable colleges or organisations related to the particular therapy and ask for details of practitioners in your area. (See the appendix for details.)

2. No ethical therapist is going to object to talking to you before commencing treatment. In this way you can find out whether the therapy concerned is suitable for your particular condition, what the cost per session will be, how many sessions you are likely to need and so on. (Beware of those therapists who seek to charge you for a complete course of treatment at the very beginning, as it is almost impossible to know how well each individual will respond and therefore how many sessions will be needed.)

3. Try not to start out with too many fixed ideas of what is going to happen. Remember that a complementary practitioner will be treating *you* rather than a single symptom.

4. No therapist has a magic wand and many forms of complementary treatment involve cooperation between practitioner and patient – either by way of 'homework' or of keeping a note of any changes which may occur – so do be prepared to play your part.

The major therapies

Acupuncture: involving the insertion of specially-made needles into specific points of the body. (And before you shudder at the thought, may I, as someone who has been on the receiving end, assure you that it does not hurt. The needles are so fine and delicate that, in the hands of a skilled acupuncturist, there need be no pain at all.) This form of Oriental medicine has its origins several thousand years ago and is effective in the holistic treatment of people suffering from many different conditions ranging from smoking to depression, as well as a range of physical disorders.

Alexander Technique: requiring anything up to twenty sessions with a trained teacher, this technique (named after its originator F. M. Alexander) concentrates on the correct alignment of the body which, in turn, leads to the elimination of physical and mental stresses. Although the number of lessons needed may make it quite an expensive form of treatment, nonetheless it is very effective and many long-standing ills may be cured by its use.

Aromatherapy: massage with essential oils made from natural sources and blended with a neutral base, such as sweet almond oils. This can be extremely beneficial in stress-related cases. A qualified aromatherapist, having done a detailed diagnosis, should be able to blend an oil specially for you. This therapy is often used in conjunction with others.

Chiropractic: a form of treatment which concentrates on the mechanical problems of the joints – particularly the spine – and the effects of those problems on the body's central nervous system and organs. This means that it is not only effective for those who suffer from spinal disorders but in the treatment of many other conditions too.

Herbalism: a holistic treatment involving the use of herbal remedies specifically chosen and blended for different conditions. The remedy does not, as many people think, have to be taken in liquid form as a tea or medicine. There are many other methods including capsules, poultices and oils.

Homoeopathy: developed from the natural law 'similia similibus curantur (like should be cured by like)'. This involves the use of remedies (usually in tablet form) which are designed to stimulate the patient's own natural healing ability. A qualified homoeopath will have studied for at least three years and will spend a great deal of time in compiling a detailed history of the patient, including character, antecedents, likes and dislikes and so on.

Hypnotherapy: involving the state of heightened suggestibility brought about by means of hypnosis. However, this does not mean, as many people assume, that the patient loses knowledge of what is taking place or the power to exert his or her own will. Though often believed to be most beneficial for those who wish to give up smoking or to lose weight, hypnotherapy has, in fact, a multitude of uses – ranging from the comparatively minor (for example, breaking the nail-biting habit) through dealing with phobias, migraine, pre-menstrual problems and so on, to the severe, such as the physical results of a stroke, the symptoms of multiple sclerosis or some cases of cancer.

Iridology: this is a method of diagnosis involving detailed observation of the iris of the eye. A qualified iridologist can identify about 200 different iris markings, each one of which relates to a different area or organ of the body. Although iridology is used primarily as a means of detecting problems before other symptoms appear rather than as a way of treating those problems, many iridologists are also herbalists or homoeopaths and can go on to work towards effecting a cure.

Massage: therapeutic massage is an excellent way of inducing relaxation and reduction of stress. In addition, particularly when combined with manipulation, it reduces muscle tension which in turn lessens the activity in the central nervous system. In conjunction with the technique of manual lymph drainage, massage can help the body to get rid of harmful toxins which may have accumulated. There are also, of course, emotional and spiritual benefits to be reaped simply from the healing touch of another person's hands.

Naturopathy: a system of medicine involving different natural methods which help to stimulate the body's vital force. The body has the ability to heal itself by means of its vital force and, according to the principles of naturopathy, disease is the resistance of that vital force to abnormal conditions in the body. Because this treatment is a holistic therapy, the person as a whole will be treated rather than a specific problem area and this treatment often involves a combination of techniques, such as dietary therapy, water treatment, hot or cold water packs and massage.

Reflexology: involving massage of the feet (and sometimes the hands) to induce a therapeutic effect. The body is divided into zones, each one of which relates to a corresponding zone on the underside of the foot. By exerting gentle pressure on the zones of the foot the reflexologist is able to diagnose areas of malfunction in the body and then, by massage of the appropriate area of the foot, to help the body heal itself by improving the functioning of the nervous and circulatory systems. It is beneficial not only in cases of physical disease but also where there is extreme stress or tension.

Shiatsu: a form of healing involving pressure on acupuncture points using thumbs, palms of the hands and fingers – as well as sometimes elbows and knees. This treatment, which originated in Japan, is by no means as violent as it sounds and it can be used, in varying degrees, on anyone from babies to the very old. It helps muscular relaxation and improves circulation. It can also reduce stiffness and increase mobility when practised by an experienced therapist.

Yoga: yoga therapy is designed to rectify that imbalance in our inner selves from which most of us suffer and which causes tension in the body and the mind. The patient is taught to control the activities of his or her mind and – as the mind governs the body – this can play a vital part in healing. Although the whole life-style will be taken into consideration, this therapy does not necessarily involve drastic changes. It also includes the use of meditation and visualisation techniques.

As all the therapies mentioned above are holistic in nature, you may be delightfully surprised to find that not only do you recover from whatever was ailing you but you also improve your general level of health and well-being. And because holism involves every aspect of the individual, you will not only feel better physically but you are likely to be more alert, freer from stress, more able to interact well with others and able to find greater peace of mind. A list of benefits which would make the cost of whichever treatment you choose well worthwhile.

PART II

The Emotional Self

3

How Your Emotions Affect You

KNOW YOURSELF

As human beings we consist not only of physical bodies but of minds, emotions and spirits too. And any one of these elements can adversely affect the effective functioning of the others.

If you have ever doubted the effect of our emotions on our physical state, just think of some of the phrases in common usage. We talk of shaking with anger, trembling with fear, glowing with satisfaction – and these expressions are usually to be taken literally; we do, in fact, display our emotions in such ways. When we are in love, we say that our hearts are 'racing' – and, indeed, they often do. We also speak of being 'consumed' with guilt and, although we are not literally eaten away, the phrase is not so very far from the truth when you consider the harmful effect guilt can have on the physical body.

And yet so many people are pleased with the way they manage to hide their emotions – to maintain that 'stiff upper lip' of which men in particular seem to be so proud. If only those people realised the harm they are doing to their health by not allowing themselves to show what they really feel – sometimes not even admitting those feelings to themselves – perhaps they would unbend a little.

This section of the book is designed to help you come to terms with your deepest emotions and the people or events which may have caused them in the first place. But, before you can find a solution, you first have to realise that a problem exists.

Look at the list of statements below and see which, if any, apply to you on a regular basis. Don't worry too much about the occasional hiccup in your emotional state – it is the repetitive pattern we are looking for.

Emotional Checklist:

I do my best to hide my real feelings from others
I always try to please other people
I am lacking in self-confidence
I am shy when faced with people I do not know
I find it hard to believe that someone can really care for me
'A place for everything and everything in its place' is my motto
Decision-making is something I find difficult
I don't like to touch or be touched
Crying (myself or other people) embarrasses me
I feel guilty if I'm not busy
I get bored easily
Much of my time is spent doing things I don't enjoy
I try to avoid conflict where possible
I often feel impatient or frustrated
I find it hard to laugh out loud
Making friends is very difficult
I feel stupid if I cry at an emotional film or book
It is impossible to relax
I never have time to enjoy myself
I don't allow myself to get angry
Humour and sex have nothing to do with each other
'Anything for a quiet life' is my philosophy
I sometimes feel like running away from it all
I don't like to complain about bad service or shoddy goods

If three or more of the above statements regularly apply to you, you probably need to think about your emotions

and the effect they are having on the other aspects of
your life.

WHY STIFLED EMOTIONS CAN CAUSE PHYSICAL HARM

Emotions which are stifled or suppressed involve holding
yourself permanently in check and this is bound to cause
tension. It is well established that tension and stress can
cause a variety of physical problems, ranging from
attacks of influenza through to heart attacks, strokes and
even cancer.

What happens when you become tense? Your muscles
tighten up, your heart beats faster, your blood pressure
rises and your body produces extra adrenalin to help
you cope with the stressful situation. That is all very
well if you have an emergency to deal with – you will
need those reactions to help you get through it. But
when this state of tension is almost permanent and you
do nothing to counteract it, those physical problems are
likely to arise.

When you relax and 'switch off' this tension the body
returns to normal. Your heart and pulse rate slow down
again, your blood pressure drops, your muscles relax
and the production of adrenalin reduces. For women in
particular, this last effect is particularly important as,
when the body is producing an excess of adrenalin, it is
not capable of producing as much of the female hormones as is normally desirable. When you are approach-
ing your period these are the hormones which help to
reduce the amount of discomfort (physical and
emotional) that you feel. This is the reason for the high
incidence of pre-menstrual tension among women who
find it particularly difficult to relax or unwind.

Babies are not born suffering from chronic guilt, anger
or any other of the destructive emotions. These have to
be brought about as a result of things which happen
during life. And, of course, all sorts of things do happen
to us as we grow. Some of these things are done to us
deliberately while others are the unintentional actions of

others or unavoidable events. Naturally, we cannot always choose what happens to us but, once we have reached adulthood, we can choose how much we let those happenings affect us.

There is an old song which says you should 'accentuate the positive and eliminate the negative'. In other words, you have to increase and develop the positive sides of your emotional self and do your best to counteract any destructive elements.

There are five very important negative emotions (as well as many lesser ones). Let's look at the five in turn and see how they apply to you and what you can do to counteract any harmful effects they may be having on your life.

ELIMINATE THE NEGATIVE

1. Anger

Anger is a natural emotion and, provided it is dealt with sensibly, it need not do any permanent harm. Indeed, one of the worst things you can do with anger is suppress it. This can result in many physical problems from indigestion (caused by the flow of excess acid into the stomach) to the high blood pressure, strokes and even heart attacks caused by the reactions described earlier.

Suppression of anger also brings about other symptoms such as headaches and insomnia. And the medical profession is now beginning to accept that those who constantly suppress their anger are more likely to develop cancer than those who are able to express it.

What to do about anger

* When you feel anger welling up within you, ask yourself whether or not it is justified. It you feel that it is, perhaps because of some injustice or a hurtful act, *do something about it*. If, however, you are just observing an

aggressive attitude on the part of someone else, what is to be achieved by allowing it to make you angry? Are you capable of letting it go and walking away? If so, that is fine, but remember that walking away only works if you are able to dismiss the incident or attitude. It will do no good at all if it leaves you fuming internally for the rest of the day.

* If you feel that your anger is justified, what are you going to do about it? Perhaps you need to make a complaint or let your feelings be known. You don't always have to shout and scream to prove that you are angry; indeed, this will often make the other person defensive and you will never be able to get through to them. You must make your point firmly and say that you are angry about the situation. If you simply store everything inside you, nothing will ever change. Not only will the situation which upsets you continue, but you will continue to do yourself harm by fuming about it.

* If you feel anger growing inside you, it is a good idea to do something physical. No, I don't mean punch the other person on the nose – apart from the fact that you will simply prolong or exacerbate the aggression, you will probably hurt your hand! But do something to get rid of your own aggressive feelings. Try digging the garden, thumping the pillow or even screaming (though not where you'll frighten the baby or the cat) – you will feel much better for it.

2. Grief

Of course there are going to be times in your life when you feel sad or unhappy and, at such times, it is perfectly natural to cry. Unfortunately many people look on the shedding of tears as a sign of weakness. As children grow older they are usually told that it is 'babyish' to cry. Little boys, in particular, are taught to suppress their tears and to maintain their composure at all costs. But crying is healthy. I am not suggesting that you should collapse in a soggy heap if you bang your head or shut your finger in the door; but suppressing tears when you are really unhappy is suppressing the grief itself and this can be harmful in several ways:

* Crying provides a valuable emotional outlet. Even though it may do nothing to alter the circumstances, many people feel much calmer and more able to cope with the situation after 'a good cry'.
* Shedding tears is a way of letting other people know that you are in need of comfort. When we are babies we cry so that our parents will pick us up and cuddle us. Just because we grow older, it doesn't mean that we are not just as much in need of comfort from those around us.
* Tears actually contain protein and they are a means of ridding the body of potentially harmful chemical wastes. If you never cry, you will simply retain those wastes within your body.

What to do about grief

* If you are sad and feel the need to cry, go ahead and do so. You may well find yourself surprised at the reactions of other people. They are unlikely to be embarrassed or contemptuous; it is a natural human instinct to want to comfort someone who is obviously unhappy. So, even if those around you cannot change the situation which is causing your grief, they can give you the warmth, love and compassion you so badly need.
* Don't be surprised if your grief manifests itself in unexpected ways. You may have reached a stage where you feel you have 'got over' the original cause of your sorrow and even find yourself able to talk calmly about it to others. Suddenly you might find yourself crying more than usual over a sad – or even a happy – television programme, book or film.
* Try not to criticise a child who is showing grief. This is particularly relevant in the case of boys – somehow society seems to think it is appropriate for little girls to shed tears but is embarrassed when a young boy reacts in the same way. Remember that a child can be just as

upset by the death of a beloved animal as by a human so do your best not to trivialise their grief at such times. * Allow your children to see your own grief so that they grow up with the idea that it is a natural reaction to an unhappy situation.

3. Guilt

Guilt comes in all shapes and sizes. One person may feel guilty because 'I shouldn't have eaten that chocolate bar' while the next is suffering pangs because of some pain caused to another person. We feel guilty about sins of commission and sins of omission – when we have done something we shouldn't or when we have not done something we should.

One of the most destructive of all emotions, guilt can inflict real damage upon both the physical and mental health while at the same time causing us to feel that we may have irretrievably lost our spiritual path. Taken to extremes, it will cause the person who feels inadequate to become a workaholic, compelling him to take on more and more in order to make up for his own shortcomings.

Guilt can cause you to feel that you are a failure. But there is, of course, a vast difference between failing at something and actually being a failure. The person does not exist who has not failed on more than one occasion – whether we are talking about marriage, the driving test or baking the perfect sponge. But if one failure damns us for life, there would never be a happy second marriage, a confident second-test driver or a successful birthday cake.

We all have to accept that each of us has made mistakes in the past – and, indeed, that we are going to make more in the future. Feeling guilty about such mistakes is a waste of energy. Far better to use that energy in a positive way by becoming determined not to repeat yesterday's errors but to use the experience gained to improve the situation and do things better in the future.

In fact, it is a vital part of spiritual development that such mistakes are made, for how else are we to learn and to evolve? One view is that, even though the current physical self will perish, the spirit goes on from life to life; if this is the case, one of the things that spirit has to learn is how to deal with all areas of negativity. I believe that, by the time the spirit enters the body, it has already chosen the lessons it wishes to learn and the difficulties it wishes to overcome during that lifetime. After that, there being no predestination, it is up to the human being concerned to deal with the problems as they arise – successfully or otherwise.

So, if you have done something in the past which you now regret and would do differently were the situation to repeat itself, you should be pleased that you have learned something vital and that your spirit, having dealt with that negative aspect, will not have to encounter it again.

Intention, of course, often makes a difference to the degrees of guilt experienced. After all, there is a vast difference between deliberately stamping on another person's toes and accidentally tripping over their foot. The owner of the foot may suffer just as much pain but is likely to be far more forgiving to the clumsy perpetrator than to the sadistic one. If you are suffering pangs of remorse because of some unintentional action in the past, don't you think it might be time to tell yourself that you will be more careful in the future – and let the guilt go?

Sometimes guilt is caused by other people – or even by society. What about the parent who says to their son or daughter 'You go and have a good time. Don't worry about me; I'll be all right.'? If that isn't guilt-inducing, I don't know what is. Or the person who pleads 'You would do it if you really loved me' – whatever the 'it' happens to be, the victim is likely to comply because a sense of guilt forces him or her to do so.

The kind of guilt imposed by society is responsible for maintaining a certain amount of law and order within our civilisation. It imposes on us the belief that it is wrong to steal or to commit murder – and that has to be a good thing. But what of the mini-commandments: Thou shalt not sit and watch television all evening; Thou shalt not have a lie-in on Sunday morning? As long as no one is inflicting harm on anyone else, why should they be made to feel guilty for a little self-indulgence?

Guilt, or constantly thinking back to past errors, only has any value if you are able to learn from it and to make a firm decision to avoid those errors in the future. But do remember that, without mistakes, we would never progress. Think of the toddler learning to walk and how often he falls down only to pick himself up and try again. Perhaps there is much that we can learn from observing our children.

Women are the world champions when it comes to feeling guilty. And there are so many more opportunities for guilt in our present civilisation. Whether to marry or pursue a career; when to have children – or, indeed, whether to have them at all; whether and when to return to work after the children are born; whether to continue working or stay at home and look after an aged relative – the problems for today's woman are endless. On many occasions the guilt caused by these problems is exacerbated by the opinions of others – from well-meaning friends and relatives to the views of media 'experts'.

Men too suffer the pangs of guilt – although they have not yet become as expert as women. And it is often the man who is both sensitive and caring who is made to suffer the most. Such a man may be delighted to become a father yet he will not wish to think that he is depriving his partner of her career – even temporarily. And if he willingly takes on his share of household and parental duties, he may still have to contend with the scorn expressed by some old-fashioned 'macho' types who would not dream of being seen to do what they continue to think of as 'women's work'.

What to do about guilt

* If some past incident is causing these feelings of guilt within you, take a look at precisely what happened. Was the incident the result of some deliberate action on your part? If it was, all you can do is try to make amends if this is possible, learn by your mistakes and decide not to make them again.

* Many people feel guilty after the loss of a loved one – perhaps because of something they said or something they did not say. So many times I have heard someone tell me how they wished they had told the person now dead how much they loved them. But you can still do so. Just because that person is not sitting here beside you does not mean they cannot hear your words or understand what is in your heart. If you have any belief in God and a life hereafter (or whatever other words you may use for that concept), then surely that is the one place where there has to be true forgiveness. And if God can forgive, who are you to say that forgiveness is wrong? If you can be forgiven, surely you can learn to forgive yourself.

* If your guilt is caused by the attitude of someone else – 'It was all your fault!' – ask yourself whether that person's attitude is justified. If you truly feel that it is not, then it is probably some inadequacy on the part of your accuser which causes him to think as he does.

* If you are one of those women who feels guilty about the marriage/home/work situation, sit down and decide what is right for you and those closest to you. If your actions or way of life are, in fact, the ones which seem best and most appropriate, then do ignore all other opinions. No one else has the right to tell you how to live your life or to suggest that your decisions are wrong. Many of those women who choose to stay at home and bring up their children are made to feel guilty by outsiders (often in the media) implying that they 'should' be working. Conversely, those who decide to return to work very soon after having a baby get the message that they are neglecting their child. If you have made a choice and are happy with it, then it is no one else's concern and you should not allow yourself to suffer from externally-imposed guilt.

4. Anxiety

Babies do not enter this world suffering from anxiety; it is a condition which is imposed upon them by other people – although not necessarily intentionally. The kindest and most loving parents may be so protective of their child that they cause that child to be anxious and over-cautious from a very early age. Of course a certain amount of caution is necessary, for how else is the child to learn that he should not put his hand in the fire or stick his finger into an electric socket? But it is the parent who is forever admonishing the infant to 'be careful' who is more likely to instil fear into the young mind.

There are also those adults who unwittingly transmit their own fears to their children. The mother who speaks with obvious dread about a forthcoming visit to the dentist may be responsible for unintentionally passing on that fear to her child. The person who is terrified of storms, while restraining him or herself from hiding in the hall cupboard, will still give off an aura of anxiety to a child who will then come automatically to associate fear with the sound of thunder.

The anxious individual becomes an expert at putting himself down. He (or she) feels that no one could possibly like or appreciate him and that he has nothing to offer. In many cases he will try to over-compensate by rushing around doing things for others as if to prove to himself that he is needed.

Perhaps his anxiety leads him to be excessively shy and almost apologise for his existence. He may even live the kind of life he does not really like simply because he feels that because everyone else is so much wiser than he is they must know best about what is right for him.

Deep anxiety may cause obsessive behaviour, fanaticism or a strict adherence to religion for the wrong reasons. Any individual is entitled to follow any faith he chooses – or even none at all – but this should be done sincerely and not simply as some sort of 'insurance policy' against whatever may arise in the future.

Taken to extremes, what begins as an anxiety may develop into a full-blown phobia, crippling the life of the sufferer. Phobia sufferers often find themselves virtual prisoners in their own home, unable to do those things which other people class as ordinary. A phobia about birds, for example, may not sound so terrible – after all you don't have to keep chickens or buy a budgie – but when you are terrified to leave your house (or even go into your own garden) in case a sparrow or a robin comes too close, your life can become a total misery.

What to do about anxiety

* If you feel inadequate or less worthy than other people, try this very simple exercise. Draw a line down the middle of a sheet of paper. On one side list all the things about yourself that you like; on the other put all the things you do not like. (I would suggest that you do this over a few days as the list may well vary according to the mood you are in.) If you find that the list of 'don't likes' is very long and there is nothing on the other side to counteract it, you are not telling the truth. Everyone has some quality they like, even if it is just that you are kind to animals.

Once you are satisfied that your list is complete, look at all those qualities that you like about yourself. If you knew someone else with the same attributes, you would feel they must be quite a nice person really, wouldn't you? Now look at the other list and see which the points listed there are changeable. (If you are 5 feet 4 inches, there is no point in wishing that you were six inches taller.) What can you do about the ones which can be changed? Can you do it yourself or do you need outside help? Decide on three things about yourself that you would like to change and tackle them calmly one at a time. The fact that you have thought things through instead of just feeling totally inadequate and that you are trying to do something about it should help you feel more positive.

* Are you shy? Do you find it impossible to speak out, whether in a work or social situation? Do you think that other people consider you boring? Why not try and turn

your thoughts outwards and see if there is someone else in the same position as yourself – what can you do to help that person feel more comfortable? Sometimes the fact that you are doing something concrete to help someone with whom you can empathise can help you to forget your own personal misgivings.

Set yourself small goals which are within your reach. Perhaps you would like to learn a new skill, rekindle an interest in a former hobby – or simply try and make that new girl at the office feel more at ease. Each time you reach a goal your attitude towards yourself will change, however imperceptibly, until you find your confidence growing. Be like the alcoholic who is trying to overcome his addiction and take one day at a time.

* If you suffer from a phobia, you would probably do best to seek outside help from a professional. It is not wise simply to ignore your fear or to force yourself to confront some object or event which terrifies you. Using hypnotherapy, the majority of phobia sufferers can be helped to overcome their anxiety in no more than four or five sessions.

* Ask yourself 'what is the worst that can happen?' in any given situation. Supposing that 'worst' were to occur – you missed that promotion, your lover rejected you, you failed to sell your house – what would be the ensuing results and how would you deal with them? Though you may not want the negative situation to arise and though you may do your best to avoid it, once you know what the worst possible outcome would be and that you could cope with it, a great deal of the anxiety is removed. And if the worst does not arise – anything else must be better and therefore easier to handle!

5. Boredom

Boredom and frustration are just as stressful as too much rushing around. The teenager who cannot find a job, the young mother with no one but toddlers to talk to, the active man forced to retire because of age regulations, the person who spends day after day doing the same repetitive work – all these people, and many others, may suffer from extreme boredom.

Now of course you may not be able to do anything to change the basic situation – you can't very well turn the children out onto the street or walk out on a job just because it is tedious. But each week consists of 168 hours; you have to work, sleep, and eat but surely it must be possible to find one or two hours somewhere in there just for you.

A sense of boredom may cause feelings of inferiority in the sufferer. The young mother may feel that she has nothing to offer – after all, much as she loves her children, their conversation may be less than stimulating. The man or woman who has been made redundant may begin to feel that life is all but over.

Because of the stress that such feelings may cause, their physical health is at risk just as much as it is in the case of the busy executive trying to cram 200 hours-worth of activity into those 168. And because a bored person has more time to think about himself and his problems, those physical results of stress may well progress more rapidly in him than in the person whose mind is always on other things.

What to do about boredom

* If you find you have too much time on your hands, take up a new interest – or even more than one. It doesn't have to be expensive – it doesn't cost much to go for a walk, work in the garden or learn to draw. In fact, if money is a problem, you may even find an outlet which is both interesting *and* profitable.
* For the mother of toddlers or babies, you may have plenty to do during the day but your mind needs stimulating too. If you cannot leave your children with anyone, find someone else in the same position as yourself and take the babies with you. You and your companion can learn French, practise yoga – or simply have a coffee and a chat. But you will have an opportunity to talk to

another adult and this will help remind you that you have just as much to offer as anyone else.

* If you live alone and are able to get out, there are many voluntary organisations just crying out for helpers. There are clubs to join, local sports centres to visit. If you are unable to leave your home, perhaps you could become a pen pal – it can open up a whole new world.

* Should you feel that you are stagnating in your abyss of boredom, use your mind by studying something which has always interested you instead of something you needed to know in order to keep your job.

* Do you feel you need a bit of excitement in your life? Then go out and find it! Perhaps you have always wanted to go up in a hot air balloon, appear on stage in a local amateur production or jump from a higher board at the swimming pool – well, how about it?

* If you really feel that there is no opportunity in your life for you to do any of the things mentioned (or anything else which appeals to you), try using your imagination. Recall pleasant experiences from the past – not with regret but with pleasure. As someone once told me 'The best things to have are memories; no one can ever take them away from you.' And you can always fantasise. You may not be able to afford that trip to a South Sea Island with its blue skies, its sandy beaches and its glorious sunshine. But you can use your imagination and take yourself on the fantasy voyage of your choice.

ACCENTUATE THE POSITIVE

1. Optimism

You must have heard the old story about the bucket of water; when it was shown to the optimist he described it as being 'half full' while the pessimist said that it was 'half empty'. Same bucket – two different outlooks.

Of course it would be unusual to be permanently in an optimistic state of mind, but who do you think gets more pleasure out of life?

Let us suppose the Smith family have planned a picnic

in the country in a few days time. Mr Smith – a pessimist – starts to worry in case it rains, the car breaks down, they are plagued by insects or one of the children gets lost. Mrs Smith, however, envisages a glorious sunny day, delicious food, fresh country air and time to relax with her husband and children. However the day turns out, she will already have enjoyed the prospect and had the excitement of looking forward to a pleasurable outing. Whereas, even if nothing goes wrong at the weekend, Mr Smith will have made himself miserable for days in advance. What a waste!

Both optimism and pessimism are highly infectious so it is possible to affect the mood of an entire group – just as throwing a stone into the water causes ripples to spread far and wide. The attitude you project therefore returns full circle back to you.

How to increase optimism

* Start at the very beginning of the day. (Well, all right, I'll allow you to be a bit bleary-eyed for ten minutes or so.) Look out of the window; there's always something good to see, whether it is the early morning sunshine, the flowers in the garden or the birds in the trees. Even the rain is good for the gardens and the farms. When you have your bath or shower, be aware of the feeling of the water on your body, the creaminess of the soap or lotion on your skin.

* Find something to look forward to; it does not have to be a major event. Perhaps you are going on an outing or meeting a friend. Optimistic anticipation can be a great source of pleasure.

* Try looking at things from a different viewpoint. If you are stuck in a boring job, concentrate on the fact that it is providing money for your needs and your pleasures and that it gives you a measure of independence. If you spend your time at home looking after small children, you can have the pleasure, within reason, of arranging your daily timetable to suit yourself. You can find ways of taking advantage of good weather while others are

shut in stuffy offices. You are also responsible for the formation of future adults and, although children may not seem terribly appreciative at the time, most of them, when grown up, look back with delight on simple childhood memories.

* While there is much joy to be gained from happy memories, don't waste time looking back on things which have caused you pain or distress. There is nothing you can do to change what has gone before and you will only cause yourself misery in the present if you concentrate on the gloomier aspects of the past.

* Make a list of all those things which make life worth living – such as friends, relations, pets, the view from the window, your favourite radio programme.

* Don't tell yourself 'I would be happy if only . . . I were rich/beautiful/married.' Try being happy now – it's catching, so other people are far more likely to seek your company.

2. Love

Love is the most positive emotion of all. It affects not only our emotional well-being but our physical condition too. If you doubt this, think of those patients who have slipped into a coma and who are awakened when those who love them have spent time with them, talking to them, touching them, playing their favourite music.

There are many kinds of love and each one is important. There is the love we feel for a husband, wife or lover. We love our children and our friends. We love our pets. We love mankind. Every sort of love has a value of its own and the wonderful thing is that there is a limitless supply if we care to call upon it. And it is something of which we cannot give or receive too much.

Love is healing and healing is love. Although we will go on to think about what is commonly thought of as spiritual healing in a later section of this book, true healing is all around us. Think of the mother whose child has just fallen over and grazed his knee – what does she do? She kisses it better. And somehow it *is* better. Her love for her child has given him comfort and helped him forget his pain.

Recently it has been found that those old people who either have pets of their own or who have access to animals are often actually healthier – and are certainly happier – than those who have no such contact. However old or ill one might be, there is something healing and comforting about stroking the soft fur of a purring cat or looking into the trusting eyes of a faithful dog.

Psychiatric research has found that children who are deprived of physical demonstrations of love are far more likely to manifest behaviour problems and to grow into emotionally unbalanced adults, unable themselves to give or receive any kind of love or warmth.

How to make the most of love

* It is easy to think that those we love are well aware of that fact. Perhaps they are. But they need more. They need to be *shown* that we love them. Never be afraid to touch those you love most. So much can be conveyed by putting your arms around someone's shoulders or giving them a kiss.
* Remember also to tell them that you love them. A man I know told me that he was twenty years old before he realised that his mother really loved him. An undemonstrative woman, the mother was quite incapable of putting her arms around her son and telling him that she was proud of him or that she loved him. When the young man was twenty he discovered that his mother had been boasting about how wonderful he was to all her friends. But how sad that she had not been able to say that to the one person who really longed to hear it.
* Love does not involve giving fancy parcels tied up with big red bows. Love is giving your time to the person for whom you care. Great joy can come from doing things together and from real communication.
* Remember that, where love is concerned, the more you give the more you get. Whether we are talking about a man and woman offering their love to one another or

mankind in general showing its love to the planet as a whole, that love will be repaid many times over.

3. Joy

I have deliberately used the word 'joy' here rather than the word 'happiness'. Happiness, wonderful as it is, is a transient thing, often lasting no more than a few moments. Whereas joy, described by the dictionary as 'intense gladness', can be far longer-lasting.

Many things may cause you to be joyful. And material riches do not come into it. Of course we all need sufficient to live on – and it is hard to be joyful if those basic needs are not met – but, however trite it may sound, there is much joy to be found in a spring day, the expression on a baby's face or the touch of a loved one's hand.

Laughter is really very good for you. Not simply because it shows that you are enjoying yourself at that moment but because it actually contributes to your physical and mental health. Laughter provides exercise for your heart and your lungs; it reduces your blood pressure and is responsible for the release of healing hormones.

Even if you hold some position of great authority, you don't have to be solemn all the time. In fact, the more serious your role, the more you need to unwind and let yourself go when the time is appropriate.

Don't wait for life to wave its magic wand and make you joyful. Start now! Live for the present and the good things which are going to happen. By all means make plans for tomorrow but try not to spend so much time engrossed in those plans that you forget to live today. Just as there are too many people who feel guilty if they are doing nothing, there are far too many who seem to feel guilty if they are joyful.

How to increase joy

* Think back to when you were very young. What made you joyful then? Where are those things now – have you simply forgotten to acknowledge them?
* Everyone has problems – some far more than others. But, however great the problems in your life, try to find something to be joyful about. It is often the person facing the greatest difficulties who is capable of feeling joy in life. I remember visiting a hospice for the terminally ill and being struck by the peace, joy and laughter which abounded among both patients and carers. If they can do it, surely we can.
* Remember that you are partially responsible for joyfulness in other people. Like love, the more joy you are able to pass on to those around you, the more you will receive in return.
* Live in the present. You cannot change what has gone and, although you can plan for the future, it is not entirely within your control. Enjoy today – life is not a dress rehearsal.
* Do what you can to create joy around you. Smiles are catching, you know.
* Be spontaneous in the way that children are. We all have so many responsibilities in life that it is easy to forget how to have fun.
* It is not a bad idea to say 'thank you' every now and then for the good things in your life. Whether you believe you are saying those words to God, fate or life itself, they will help to bring to mind those things for which you can be grateful and this in turn will help to increase your own state of joy.

4

Relationships

Many people, on hearing the word 'relationships', think only of the interaction between one man and one woman. But we have relationships of many different sorts – with our children, our parents, our boss and our friends to name but a few. And nowhere in our lives do more problems seem to arise than in the area of relationships – and no other problems seem to have such a long-lasting effect.

Babies and toddlers

Everyone wishes to have the ideal relationship with their children yet dealing with a baby is often a particularly trying exercise for the parents. If it is a first baby, then both mother and father are inexperienced and are learning how to cope with the demands of the new infant as well as with the disruption in their own lives. The new mother is often terrified of making a mistake but she does not really know what is the best thing to do. Should she pick up the baby whenever it cries or leave it until it settles of its own accord? Should she feed her child on demand or stick to a rigid timetable? There is no 'correct' answer to such questions. What the mother finally decides to do will probably result from the opinion of someone else – whether that someone is her own mother, the local midwife or whichever childcare expert happens to be in vogue at the time. But the basic uncertainty in the mother may well transmit itself to the child and the relationship between the two of them could be off to a shaky start.

In the case of a second or subsequent baby, not only is the same amount of care necessary, but the needs of older children have to be dealt with too. The mother herself may be far more relaxed with her new infant and better able to cope by relying on her own intuition combined with the experience she has already gained. But, instead of being able to sit back and enjoy this baby, she has also to look after the other children who may only just have left the baby stage themselves. Her day will probably be crammed with essential tasks; an older child may well be feeling jealous and therefore be in need of more attention than usual; money may be in short supply – and time certainly will be.

Today's new mother may well find herself facing the additional difficulty of coping alone with her new-born infant – whether due to choice or circumstance. And we can no longer rely on the extended family being close at hand. Gone are the days when Grandma lived down the road and Auntie Maud was just around the corner, each of them providing a comforting and experienced shoulder for the young mother to lean upon.

So just at the time when that first vital relationship between parent and child is in its most tenuous stages, external tensions and difficulties are most likely to take their toll and may cause the baby to become fractious and the parent to be over-tired and irritable.

The child

In addition to all the other things the child is experiencing, this is an essential learning-time when it comes to forging relationships. Until now, in most cases, the child will only have come into contact with those who are most concerned for his welfare – mother, father, grandparents and so on. But now he has to face all those people in the great big world to whom he is just another person, starting quite often with his own brothers and sisters.

If he (and of course this applies to girls too) is the oldest child in the family, he will have had the opportunity to be the centre of attention for some time. Of course he will feel jealous when a new baby arrives on the scene – even if he does his best not to show it. How well he is able to cope with the situation will depend partly on his age at the time and partly on how carefully the adults around him handle the situation. Tempting as it may be for the harassed mother to jump at the chance of sending her three year old to playschool every morning, imagine the devastating effect this can have when it coincides with the arrival in the home of a brand new baby. The young child will feel that he is being pushed out of the way to make room for someone much more important.

The younger child has to form a relationship with older children in the family. He may have to put up with being ordered about by a big brother or sister anxious to exert their authority. Depending upon the attitude of his parents, he may begin to feel that he is either far more or far less important than the other children of the family and this too will affect his relationship with them.

Then comes the brand new world of school where new relationships are formed which belong to the child alone and are not necessarily anything to do with other members of the family. He comes into close contact with both a teacher and other children of his own age and many of his future feelings about himself will result from what happens to him at this time.

The early life of a child and the attitudes of those around him can have a dramatic effect upon his adult emotional state. The loving parent who tries to shield the child from harm to such an extent that he becomes timid and anxious can cause as many problems as the thoughtless and impatient adult who thinks that telling the child he is stupid will spur him on to greater efforts. Unless something is done to reverse the effect of such early programming, the former child will grow up to be nervous and unsure while the latter is likely to have no confidence in himself whatsoever.

Children tend to believe that those adults around them are all-wise and all-powerful and it follows that whatever these adults say *must* be true. If what they say is derogatory, then that opinion (false or unfair as it may be) will be registered in the child's subconscious mind and will grow and expand as he approaches adulthood.

The adolescent

The adolescent is emerging from the small and comparatively cushioned world to which he has belonged and is having to face a great deal of pressure from many different relationships. As the influence of his family dwindles, the effect upon him of his contemporaries increases. Many a teenager has been drawn into behaviour he would rather have avoided simply because he finds himself unable to stand up to his peers or to be the one who is 'different'. When the outcome of such influence is some rather high-spirited behaviour no great harm is done but unfortunately peer pressure has also led in many instances to experimentation with alcohol, drugs and glue-sniffing.

Teenagers frequently appear to be resentful of parents or teachers but in reality this is often a sign that they are testing authority and seeing just how far they can go. It is a particularly difficult time for many as, on the one hand, they are being urged to make decisions about their future while, on the other, they are expected to toe the line both at home and at school. And all this at a time when they are undergoing dramatic changes both physically and emotionally – changes which they often find very difficult to deal with.

The young adult

Now we come to a time when relationships can give extreme joy or extreme pain. The young man or woman may become involved in love affairs which are happy or unhappy and each such relationship will have a dramatic effect. Eventually (in many cases) the stage is reached where a commitment is made and a long-term partnership begins. This then results in a new set of relationships with the family of the potential partner.

At this time too there are relationships to be forged with employers and co-workers and, since such a large part of life is spent at the workplace, the good or bad effects of such relationships are likely to affect the individual's home life too.

With marriage or change of job may come a move to an entirely new district and the need to form relationships with new neighbours and to find new friends. Family and old friends are not necessarily forgotten but distance will naturally make frequent contact less likely and the newly formed unit will take precedence, particularly when the young adults become parents themselves and the whole process begins all over again.

The older adult

How relationships may have changed by this time! Their children have grown up, perhaps left home and, however much they may love their parents, they no longer need them in the same way. Perhaps a couple are looking at one another in a different light – it is to be remembered that one in three marriages now ends in divorce. Sometimes one partner (or both) will seek to enhance life by indulging in casual affairs but this often leads to feelings of disenchantment and guilt and does nothing whatsoever to improve the situation.

Those who have worked harder at their relationship, allowing it to change and develop (or perhaps those who are luckier – whichever way one chooses to look at it) may be content together but external relationships will still change. They may well have elderly parents who need to be cared for, whether physically or materially, and they may cause a good deal of pressure. It is not easy to come to terms with the idea that the parents on whom you depended all those years ago may now – possibly because of ill-health – have become dependent upon you.

The elderly

The greatest problem for many elderly people is that relationships tend to dwindle. Children are grown up now with lives of their own. Death or distance may have reduced the number of friends, and relationships with acquaintances may appear to be superficial.

All the relationships mentioned so far are those of the individual. But of course one can form one's own relationship with one's god or with mankind in general. And problems do not only occur in individual relationships – think of the difficulties between the Protestants and the Catholics in Northern Ireland or between black and white in South Africa.

However many problems there may be, there is a natural human instinct to form relationships all through our lives, although occasionally one will find a recluse – someone who has deliberately cut himself off from human contact. Even those who have entered a deeply religious life where it may appear that they are hiding themselves away from close contact with others have in fact formed a deep and spiritual relationship with their god.

At any stage in life, we can improve our relationship with others by learning to be aware and to communicate. Communication does not necessarily involve words but can often be non-verbal too. How you look at someone, the attention you give them and your body language are all means of communication and can have a strong effect upon the recipient, even if he only perceives it on a subconscious level.

THE RELATIONSHIP BETWEEN PARENT AND CHILD

Perhaps the most important relationship of all is that between parent and child. When this is good, the child may grow up to be confident and self-assured and this will help him throughout his adult life. But if this relationship is poor, the damage done may adversely affect that child for the rest of his days. Whatever self-image we come to accept when we are very young, that is the one we seek to perpetuate by finding others to treat us as we subconsciously believe we deserve. The child who is abused or belittled will often, when an adult, seek out others who will treat him in the same way as this fits in with his inner image of himself. The child who is encouraged to be a self-respecting individual, however, will carry that impression of himself forward into adulthood and will find that others respond to him as someone worthy of their respect.

Because this relationship is so significant and its effects are so far-reaching, perhaps it would be a good idea to stop and consider what kind of parent or what kind of child you are. Answer yes or no to the statements below and see if it helps you to uncover the reasons for your family relationships – be they bad or good.

What type of parent am I?

1. I am entitled to my children's respect simply because I am their father/mother.
2. My children should do what I say without arguing.
3. All pocket money must be earned not given.
4. Rules are rules (bedtime and so on) and must be adhered to.
5. If I didn't keep on at them, homework would never get done.
6. Punishing children is harmful in the long-term.
7. Let them have fun; there is plenty of time for responsibility when they are adult.

8. I like to give my children whatever they want, even if I have to go without.
9. It's quicker for me to clear up/wash up and so on than to argue with them about doing it.

I am sure that, whatever your answers to the above questions, you love your children. However, if you have answered 'yes' to all or most of statements 1–5, it could be that you are being too strict with them, possibly causing resentment and friction. Remember that love and respect has to be earned, whether from an adult or from a child. If you want your son or daughter to grow up able to talk to you, perhaps you could consider being a little less authoritarian. Of course there have to be some rules but try and ensure that there is a good reason for them. It is far better to have fewer rules which you can insist your children keep than to insist that everything is done in accordance with strict regulations. If, from the very beginning, you are able to listen to your children's point of view and discuss things with them, they will grow up to be your friends and to respect what you say.

If, on the other hand, you answered 'yes' to all or most of statements 6–9, you are probably being too soft and permissive. Children are very quick to spot this and will take advantage of the situation – and once they know they can get away with anything, you will lose their respect. Most children like to know where they stand and, although they may argue about bedtime, homework, and so on, they prefer a fairly ordered home life, particularly when they are very young.

As you can see, it is a case of finding a happy balance between being too authoritarian and too easy-going.

What sort of son/daughter am I?

To find out whether your early life has forced a good or bad self-image upon you now that you are adult, answer yes or no to the statements below.

1. I never contradict my parents.

2. They have the ability to make me feel guilty if I don't write/'phone/visit at regular intervals.
3. I always ask their advice before important changes (moving house/changing job/marriage).
4. If their opinion differs to mine, I believe that they know best.
5. I often feel that they are disappointed in me.

If you have answered 'yes' to any of the above, then you are still being dominated by your parents to some extent. If you have answered 'yes' to three or more of them, you are probably perpetuating this self-image by looking for friends or partners who will treat you in the same way. And this situation will continue until you decide to do something to change it.

The adult/child within

Within each individual there is the adult and the child. The adult within is our inner 'authority figure' telling us that we 'should do this' or 'must not do that'. It is the judgmental and critical element of our nature. But, just as adult people have many facets to their personalities, so too does the adult within. In addition to its authoritative role, it is also capable of nurturing and of being positive, calm, reasoning and practical.

The emergence of the adult within has nothing to do with numerical age. Some people discover this element of themselves while still very young; others come to it at a much later stage in their lives – and others never manage to find it at all.

The child within can display either positive or negative characteristics – or, more usually, a mixture of the two. The positive aspects of the inner child are a sense of fun and curiosity – 'let's play and enjoy life'. The negative aspects are those portrayed by a demanding or greedy child – 'I want it; I want it *now*'.

The extent to which either the adult or child within plays a significant part in our lives depends greatly on our own upbringing. If our parents were kind and supportive, our own adult within is likely to be so. If they gave in to our tantrums, our child within will probably manifest itself in a negative, rather than a positive, fashion.

ONE PERSON – DIFFERENT FACES

Another reason for difficulties arising in relationships is that each of us has a number of different 'faces'.

Inner Face: The Inner Face is how we see ourselves. This view is not based on logic but is greatly influenced by the programming to which we have all been subject from day one of our lives. The child who has been told that he is 'useless', 'stupid' or will 'never amount to anything' will go on to become an adult whose Inner Face is that of a worthless individual – even if events prove that the truth is very different. One of my former patients, a respected scientist who had worked for many years in the field of cancer research, still kept the inferior Inner Face inflicted on him by demanding parents and a series of thoughtless teachers.

The reverse is also true. If parents have managed to instil in their child a sense of his own worth as an individual, then, whatever knocks that child may encounter as an adult, he will have the inner confidence which will enable him to pull through and make a success of his life – success in this context having nothing to do with money but with achieving one's aims as an individual, whatever they may be. The person with a healthy Inner Face is the one who is most able to form good relationships with others; he does not feel that he has to put on an act to impress yet neither does he feel superior to those with whom he comes in contact. He has the confidence simply to be himself.

Inner/Outer Face: This is the way we *think* others see us – although we may be wrong. Perhaps we think our friends see us as calm and capable while we *know* that we are secretly in a state of panic. Perhaps we believe that others perceive us as weak and ineffectual when in reality we choose to make a stand only about those things which really matter, knowing that it often takes more strength to remain calm and in control than to meet aggression with more aggression.

It is the Inner/Outer Face which causes the most heartache. The person beset by fears and anxieties who nevertheless manages to present a confident exterior will often feel self-contempt t ɔcause he feels that he is living a lie and that one day someone will catch him out. The individual who is determined to remain calm in the face of aggression, even though he may feel he is doing the right thing, might wonder whether others look down on him and be tempted to behave as others think he should.

The Outer Face: This is how other people *really* see us – and this is the Face we cannot know unless we ask those whom we trust to tell us their true opinions. And how often those opinions can really surprise us; a young woman patient who had four hearty older brothers told me that, although they always treated her well, she always felt completely insignificant beside them. Yet, when they were asked how they felt about their sister, each one of them paid tribute to her gentleness and femininity and said how much they cared for her. Wouldn't it have been sad if she had lived her life with her mistaken Inner/Outer Face?

How well do you know your own Faces? Try this experiment. List all the characteristics which make up your Inner Face – how do you perceive yourself? This is not a time for logic but for immediate reaction. You may *know* that you have passed all your exams but, if your Inner Face tells you (for whatever reason) that you are incapable of achievement, that is what you must put down.

Now make a second list under the heading Inner/Outer Face – how do you think other people (friends, family, people you work with) see you? What do you feel they think of you? The characteristics listed here may be quite different to the ones you believe you have.

The final list – the Outer Face – is a little more difficult to compile because you have to ask other people to be honest with you. And, of course, there are only a certain number of people you can approach with that request. Close friends and family – those who really care about you – will be happy to comply but you must remember to tell them that you would like them to indicate what they think are your weaknesses as well as your strengths or they will simply say nice things about you. It is far more difficult to approach someone to whom you do not feel at all close and in many cases the only way to do this is by means of a third person who may be willing to ask them for their opinion of you.

When you have all three lists completed, study them closely and see what they tell you about yourself. I think you may well be surprised by what you see. Many of those aspects of your personality which you may have perceived in a negative way might be regarded by others as positive elements of your character. Of course the reverse may be true in some cases – but at least you are now aware of which areas of yourself you might wish to change in order for your Outer Face to conform with your Inner one.

There is another very positive outcome of this exercise. Once you have learned to see the difference between your own three Faces, you are more likely to look behind the mask presented by others and to understand them better. And, of course, this type of understanding is one of the vital components of a successful relationship.

CONFIDENCE

Of all the requests made by those patients who come to consult me, the most common by far is for me to 'make them more confident'. If only it were that simple. If I had a storehouse full of confidence, I would gladly give each one of them as much as they needed. And, although it is possible to help each person to develop into a more confident individual, it is something we have to work towards together. And before we can create this new confident person, we frequently have to break down the poor self-image he or she has acquired over the years.

What is confidence? Confidence is based on self-esteem and the ability to value yourself not for what you have achieved but simply for being *you*. Many people find it difficult to realise how great a value they have even if they are not beautiful, clever or rich. Perfection has nothing to do with your worth – indeed a perfect person, if he or she existed, would probably be an extremely boring individual.

Self-esteem means feeling comfortable with yourself. Those who have it will be better at forming relationships of all sorts because they do not find it impossible to believe that other people could actually respect them and care for them.

It sounds simple, doesn't it? And for some people it is. But most of us experience periods of low self-esteem at different times and some – particularly if they have been unhappy in their early life – seem to be permanently stuck with such a poor impression of themselves and their own worth that 'self-esteem' is to them just a word which applies to other people more fortunate than themselves.

Of course, most of us feel more confident in some situations than in others. Perhaps you are fine when dealing with someone on a one-to-one basis but dread the thought of going to a party. You may be fully in control in your own home and yet be tormented by feelings of insecurity at work. If this applies to you and you find some situations more difficult than others, stop and think about those areas where your confidence appears to be at its lowest – what can you do to improve matters?

If you feel, for example, that your appearance lets you down, perhaps you could spend a little time studying magazine features to see where you could make some changes. This does not have to involve buying the expensive outfits frequently depicted in such journals but absorbing the ideas about colour, style, make-up and so on. You are unlikely to want to copy slavishly what you see in the magazines but you may choose to adapt those ideas which appeal to you in order to feel happier with the way you look.

It could be that your lack of confidence is connected with work. If so, ask yourself why this is. Are you feeling out of your depth because no one has explained things fully to you? Have you just been given a position of more responsibility? Are you perhaps in the wrong job? Or – as is very common – do you spend too much time worrying about what other people think of you? Naturally we cannot always totally ignore the views of others but, if you know you are doing your job as well as you can, remember it is your own opinion which counts.

Isolating the source of a problem indicates to you which areas you should try to change. If the difficulties arise at work, perhaps you could study in order to understand the job better. It could even be that you need to change job altogether. Or it might be that you have to learn to give yourself credit for what you are able to achieve.

It could be that your lack of confidence concerns home life; perhaps you hate people coming to see you because your home is not beautiful – or perhaps it is never tidy. The first thing to realise is that anyone who comes to visit you because they want to will not care – and probably will not notice – if your home is not perfect. They certainly will not go out of their way to be critical – and if they do they are not worth knowing in the first place! If you are really living in a mess, have a grand clear-out and put the whole place straight; after that try to discipline yourself to clean and tidy on a regular basis to keep it under control. Ask yourself whether others who live in your home are pulling their weight. It doesn't matter how young they are – even a small child can be taught to put his toys in a box every evening.

Improving your confidence may well necessitate making decisions. One of my patients (I'll call her Jane) realised that every time she visited her parents she came away feeling upset and inferior. She did not feel it would be right to cut herself off from her family altogether but she now visits them occasionally rather than every week as before. She and her husband have also learned to make a family joke out of the situation, trying to guess before each visit how many times Jane's mother will criticise her. By reacting in this way, Jane is able to stand back from the situation and it cannot hurt her as it used to do. She has not cut herself off from her parents, however, as this is something which would only have led her to feel guilty and therefore decreased her confidence even further.

You may not choose to react to situations which damage your self-esteem in the same way as Jane. We each have to find the method that suits us. But it is up to you to make some decisions, however small, and to put them into action.

Confidence boosters:

* Learn to accept yourself as you are and to know that you are allowed to have faults as well as good points;
* Think about those good points (I am well organised; I'm a caring person and so on) and give yourself as much credit as you would give someone else with those qualities;
* We all make mistakes – try and learn from yours and they will have been worthwhile. Don't keep going over them in your mind in a negative way but use the experience positively. Remember the saying 'he who never makes mistakes never makes anything worth having';
* Build on your achievements. Every time you take a step in the right direction, realise what you have done and give yourself due credit. Whether you have just passed your driving test, made your first pot of jam or walked into a room full of strangers, you have been a success. And, just as failure encourages more failure, success encourages further success;
* Pamper yourself. Set aside some time each day just for you and do whatever you like. Go for a walk, lie in the bath, listen to the radio – whatever appeals to you. You can be as active or as lazy as you wish; the important

thing is that it is something you *want* to do rather than something you feel you should do;

* Remember that it is possible to respect your own opinions *and* those of other people, even if those opinions differ. Don't alter yours to fit another person's unless the change is genuine;

* Allow your friends/family/lovers to be themselves within your shared relationship. A confident person has no need to possess another person or to monopolise their time;

* Try not to apologise too much. Instead of starting 'I'm sorry to bother you . . .' try something more positive like 'I wonder if you can help me. . .';

* Use visualisation or affirmations to help you feel better. Whether you keep yourself going (like the little engine in the children's story) by saying 'I can do it, I can do it' or whether you learn to rehearse coming events in your mind to dispel your anxieties, you can help your confidence to grow. (You will find more details of these techniques later in this book.)

Improving confidence takes time – you are not going to change your personality overnight. But start in small ways and gradually build up. You will find that the more confident you become, the more you will be able to enjoy the different relationships you have with those around you – and the happier you will be.

PART III

The Mental Self

5

Know Your Own Mind

LEFT BRAIN/RIGHT BRAIN

Did you know that your brain is divided into two sections – the left brain and the right brain? The left brain contrcls the right-hand side of the body, so that if the left brain is damaged it is the right side of the body which is paralysed. The opposite is naturally true too, the right brain controlling the left-hand side of the body.

Each person is predominantly left-brained or right-brained (although the ideal is to achieve a perfect balance). To find out which of these descriptions applies to you, place a tick by whichever of the following statements applies to you:

A. I am good at figures
   I have an analytical mind
   I think logically
   I have a sound command of language
   I enjoy scientific subjects

B. I am artistic by nature
   I tend to daydream
   I am musical or have a love of music
   I have a good visual imagination
   I have a strong sense of rhythm

If most of your ticks are against the statements in section
A, then you are predominantly left-brained; whereas if
you have placed more ticks against the section B statements, you are predominantly right-brained. Let us look
at what we know about the two halves of the human
brain:

Left brain

- connected to the right side of the body
- deals with one thing at a time
- controls verbal and mathematical functions
- deals with time
- governs the aptitude for accurate expression and use
  of language
- responsible for memory and recognition of words and
  numbers
- governs reason, logic and analysis

Right brain

- connected to the left side of the body
- can deal with several things at one time
- governs facial expression, tone of voice, body language
- controls movement, rhythm and artistic ability
- governs memory and visual recognition
- responsible for intuition and holistic thought
- related to dreams

You will see from the lists above that modern education
brings us up from early childhood to use our left brains
in preference to our right brains. How many of us, I
wonder, were told at school to 'stop daydreaming'. Now,
I do not pretend for one moment that children should
not be taught to add, subtract, read and think logically.
My only complaint is that, all too often, these skills are
taught at the expense of those natural artistic and creative
abilities the child may possess. And, just as it is unnatural to spend all one's time hopping on one leg, going

about with one eye permanently closed or trying to work with one hand tied behind the back, it is unnatural to be so unbalanced. You might cope for a while with one eye closed or one hand behind your back but you wouldn't keep it up for long – nor would you perform at maximum ability.

Just as an unused muscle grows weak in comparison to all the others, so too does an unused side of the brain. But, just as that weak muscle can be flexed, exercised and developed, you can learn to develop whichever side of your brain has been least used. It is only when the two sides are as balanced as possible that you will be able to make maximum use of your mental faculties.

And don't think that by developing the second half of your brain you will merely be doubling your mental capacity. Professor Robert E. Ornstein of the University of California, a recognised expert in left and right brain research, has proved that when you develop the second side of your brain you actually enhance your mental powers by anything from five to ten times its previous level.

MENTAL ABILITY AND AGE

At one time it was thought that the brain reached its peak of potential performance when the individual was between the ages of 18 and 25 years and that, from that time onwards, it began to deteriorate. This deterioration, it was believed, brought in its wake a lesser ability in the areas of memory, numeracy, creativity and so on. However, in his researches, Professor Mark Rosenzweig was able to prove that this was not so and that, given sufficient stimulation, the brain can actually develop at any age. Naturally this only applies where there has been no illness or injury which would cause dramatic loss of functioning. Indeed, we only have to think of such people as Einstein, Picasso, Michelangelo, Goethe and George Bernard Shaw to realise that the brain is definitely capable of functioning – and functioning to great effect – well into one's eighties or nineties.

You may have heard people speak about the loss of brain cells as we get older but, as Tony Buzan, expert in the working of the human mind, writes in his book *Make the Most of Your Mind:*

> 'even if we lose 10,000 brain cells a day from the time we are born, we have started with so many that the total number lost by the age of 80 would be less than 3 per cent.'

DEVELOPING CREATIVITY

If we accept that, so far as most people are concerned, it is the left brain which is more highly developed, what can we do to enhance the ability of the right brain and to try and become more creative? It is probable that, for a large part of our lives, little emphasis was placed on the use of imagination, colour and rhythm and yet we were all born with the potential to use our right brain just as much as the left.

The majority of people, when asked whether or not they are creative, will reply in the negative. But quite often they have not really understood the question. Most people, when the word 'creative' is used, think of artists, designers, musicians and so on. But thought itself can be creative and this creative thinking can be put to good use in all areas of life – from running a business to preparing for Christmas.

One of the great problems is that we are trained to think in lists – packing lists, shopping lists, lists of tasks to complete today . . . But lists themselves can be very limiting. Suppose, for example, you wanted to write an essay on 'Health'; you might begin by making a list of the points you wished to include. Perhaps:

Food/Drink
Exercise
Medicines
Treatment
Attitudes

– and then you might get stuck. The problem with lists is that by the time you write item number three, you have completely forgotten about item number one, and so on.

Suppose we try another method and create thought-flow charts instead of lists. To make a thought-flow chart, you begin by writing your topic in the centre and then literally allow your thoughts to flow around that topic. Let's take the same example of an essay on 'Health':

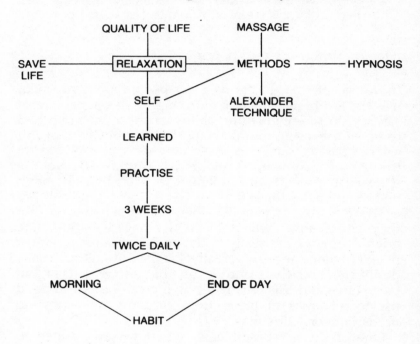

See how much more there is to think about. And you can go on almost endlessly until you have more than enough points to discuss in your essay. Indeed, you can go on until you have enough to write a book. Try it for yourself, using any topic as a starting point.

OUTSIDE INFLUENCES ON THE MIND

Many external influences can affect our state of mind, from the food we eat to the time of year, from programming in our past to stress in our current situation.

Environment

The weather situation can have a greater effect on us than many people realise. Remember how it is often difficult to think clearly when the air is heavy just before a storm, or how your mind seems to become clear and sharp in the crisp, clean air on a mountainside or beside the sea. The effect on people of different weather conditions (also known as human climatology) is taken very seriously and is being researched and studied in many parts of the world.

Dr E. Tournod of the World Health Organisation has discovered that fluctuations in weather actually bring about hormonal changes. He suggests that climatic variations almost certainly influence personal behaviour and that specific types of weather can cause an increase in anti-social behaviour in many groups, ranging from schoolchildren causing havoc in the classroom to outbreaks of violence among those taking part in mass demonstrations.

When a heatwave occurs – unless we are fortunate enough to be able to do nothing but laze around – many people become increasingly bad-tempered. And police statistics prove that motorists become more reckless and cause more problems at such times. Windy weather (as opposed to a gentle breeze) can give rise to edginess and irritability in a large proportion of the population.

Storms are responsible for many personality changes. Dr Hartwell Schulman of the Institute of Medical Climatologists has shown that just before a storm there is a reduction in atmospheric pressure which causes blood circulation to slow down. As this blood is responsible for carrying oxygen to the brain, some people are likely to become morose or depressed as a result. During the storm itself, people already ill often become worse, women nearing the end of their pregnancy may go into labour and unbalanced individuals have a tendency to become violent.

Excessive heat may make us feel 'stupid' and unable to function mentally. This is particularly true when the period of hot weather is prolonged. And yet we often find that examinations take place at the very time of year when there is most likelihood of a heatwave. It has been shown that the best time of year for such exams would be in March or April when temperatures are lower.

It is not only the weather which affects us but our surroundings too. A stuffy atmosphere, or one which is artificially heated, air-conditioned and lit, produces lethargy and depression. And yet more and more people, particularly in cities, are being forced to work in such conditions. Naturally some of these people will be more vulnerable and more susceptible to the influence of their surroundings than others but most of them will be affected to a greater or lesser degree.

Physical health

1. *Food:* As we have seen in an earlier chapter, our physical condition has a great influence on our minds and our emotions – the reverse also being true. The phrase 'a healthy mind in a healthy body' has great validity.

The food we eat has a significant effect upon our mental agility. This is not simply a case of watching the vitamins and minerals. Those doctors who have been trained to practise Ayurvedic medicine (a traditional type of Indian medicine) have been able to show that foods such as fresh vegetables, rice and pulses produce the clearest and most balanced mental state. An excess of meats and spices cause aggression while too great a consumption of dairy foods and those with a high fat content may bring about depressive tendencies and lethargy. The answer, therefore, is to maintain a diet which is as balanced and healthy as possible.

This idea of balance is just as important if you are on a reducing diet. A diet which is bizarre or extreme may bring about weight loss if strictly adhered to but, as the brain draws on its reserves to make up for the deficiency in vital nutrients, the dieter is likely to become edgy, easily upset and to experience difficulty in making decisions.

In an experiment conducted at the Mayo Clinic, a group of healthy individuals agreed to stay on a very low calorie diet for three months. At the end of that time, each one of them had experienced unpleasant symptoms; some became hostile and argumentative; some had panic attacks and nightmares; all of them found their attention span had grown shorter and they were finding it more difficult to remember things.

2. *Additives:* In recent years we have been made more aware of the danger of excessive artificial additives in our food and drink. Some of these additives cause allergies while others affect our mental agility. And nowhere is this problem more clearly seen than among our children. Because their bodies are still growing, children react more quickly to many of the things they eat. It has been shown that many additives are responsible for behavioural problems among young people, such as irritability, clumsiness, excitability and aggressiveness. In addition, they can shorten the child's attention span and make him more easily frustrated – and this in turn leads to a poorer performance in school.

3. *Drink:* It is well-known that tea and coffee contain caffeine and that caffeine is a stimulant. You might be forgiven for thinking that the absorption of a stimulant would make you better able to function mentally – but in fact this is far from the truth. Because an excess of caffeine can bring about many of the symptoms of stress and because these symptoms actually impair mental ability, you are likely to find yourself making foolish mistakes. I am not suggesting that you can never have another cup of coffee or tea but that here, as in many other areas of life, moderation is the best policy. Perhaps you could acquire a taste for decaffeinated coffee or one of the many herb or fruit teas.

Fruit squashes and many of the more popular carbonated drinks are not only high in caffeine but a large number of them also contain colouring and artificial preservatives; so too many of these will produce the same effect as an overdose of tea or coffee. Try instead to drink real fruit juice and spring or filtered water (avoiding where possible the water straight from the tap which is full of chemicals).

The dangers of excessive alcohol are perhaps more obvious and the real problem here is that the effect is cumulative rather than merely temporary. A research project carried out in 1979 showed that even people who drink moderately experience impairment of memory and this becomes greater as they age and as their consumption of alcohol increases. The significant point here is that, even when they stopped drinking, the impairment of memory remained.

Professor Noble of the University of California School of Medicine states that even two or three drinks four times a week reduces mental faculty and diminishes the ability to accomplish many different thinking tasks. Professor Noble also states that excessive alcohol can lead to premature ageing of the brain.

4. Smoking: Many reasons are currently being put forward for giving up smoking and all of them are valid. But did you realise that smoking can impair the blood which carries oxygen to the brain and therefore decrease mental efficiency? In tests carried out in both Britain and the United States it has also been proved that non-smokers have far better memory and recall than smokers. For smokers that is the bad news. The good news is that, once you have given up smoking and sufficient time has elapsed for the nicotine to clear your system, your memory and mental ability is likely to be just as good as that of someone who has never smoked.

5. Drugs: Both medically prescribed drugs and those which come under the general heading of 'non-medical substances' can cause impairment of mental faculties. Anyone who has ever taken anti-histamines to relieve an allergy or the symptoms of hay fever will know that such tablets often cause drowsiness and an inability to think as clearly as usual. Indeed, such medication usually carries a warning stating that the individual should not drive or operate machinery after taking it.

Medically prescribed drugs – essential though they may be – sometimes bring about confusion or memory loss. Even a basic antibiotic may cause feelings of depression and this in turn makes you *believe* that you remember less – although, if tested, you will probably perform as well as usual. Some people do not suffer such a reaction when taking such prescribed tablets as penicillin but, for those who do, it can often be relieved by regular eating of natural yoghourt for the duration of the course of treatment.

It is not my task here to discuss the rights and wrongs of such substances as LSD, cocaine, heroin or any other such drug. But one thing has been proved by frequent controlled tests; not only does the absorption of the substance into the system reduce the mental powers of the individual to a greater or lesser degree, but other problems arise because he *imagines* that he is actually able to function far better than usual.

6. *Injury/illness:* Even a temporary illness such as influenza can cause a 'thick head' and the inability to think clearly. And of course there are conditions such as amnesia or Alzheimer's Disease where a reduction in mental functioning is one of the predominant symptoms. But the trauma of even comparatively simple surgery can cause some people to experience short-term problems with memory and logical thought. There is even a condition known as 'intensive care psychosis' which is said to affect about twenty per cent of those who have been patients in hospital intensive care units. This condition is, fortunately, usually temporary in nature.

The shock and trauma of an accident or a physical injury may also bring about immediate inability to think clearly – even when the injury is not to the head. Concentration is diminished and reactions are often slow. For this reason it is a good idea to have emergency telephone numbers written clearly where they are easy to locate as you may not be able to remember them should the need arise.

7. *Physical exercise:* When you take regular physical

exercise your circulation improves and therefore oxygen is carried more easily and rapidly to the brain. Ask anyone who regularly runs, jogs or swims and they will tell you that, after such exercise, they experience a 'high' when their thoughts are sharper than ever, even though their muscles may ache.

Tests have been regularly carried out since the early eighties to discover whether those who exercise regularly or who have jobs which involve a considerable amount of physical exertion are able to think more clearly and remember more accurately than their IQ counterparts who lead a fairly sedentary life. The research is still continuing but conclusions to date seem to point to the fact that, although powers of reasoning are not necessarily enhanced, the speed at which the subject is able to reason or recall certainly is.

Influences of the past

Whether we like the idea or not, we have all been 'programmed' from birth by people and events around us. This programming has influenced our thinking and our pattern of ability without us knowing it. It does not have to influence our future, however, and the aware adult is quite capable of changing his ability pattern should he so desire.

Some people deliberately try to programme their children. There have been instances over the years of a child who shows signs of an advanced ability in a particular direction. Take, for example, the child who is able to deal with mathematical concepts at a very early age. He is likely to be very bright and to find learning easy but in many cases he will be coached and encouraged by a parent (usually the father) in that one direction so that he becomes a prodigy or a 'genius' at mathematics. Perhaps he will sit in a class with students five years older than he is. Perhaps he will enter university at the age of twelve. Whether he will be happy fulfilling his father's ambitions is another matter.

The same thing happens in the world of sport – and

once again it is usually the father who is the driving force. There are at least two current tennis champions who had racquets put into their tiny hands when they were no more than two or three years old. From that time onwards, when other children were out playing, they were practising their tennis and improving their game. Maybe they come to believe, when they are young adults and they receive the acclaim – and the money – which accompanies championship that it was all worth while. But maybe the day will come when they will resent the loss of their childhood years. Only time will tell.

Mental programming, of course, does not have to be quite so extreme. Nor yet does it have to be deliberate. And that programming can be either positive or negative. One of my own patients grew up in a loving family where it was assumed that he would eventually study law – just like his grandfather, his father and his uncle. No one stopped to ask the boy what he wanted, which was to study science and work in the field of research. He *did* study law and acquired all the necessary qualifications but he became increasingly depressed – a condition which was not conquered until, at the age of 28, he went back to university to study the science subjects he so loved.

Negative programming can be general or specific and, unless something is done about it at a later date, its effects can last a lifetime. 'You could never learn to speak a foreign language' one child is told, while others may frequently hear that 'You will never be as clever as your sister' or even 'You're stupid!' It doesn't matter if the child grows up to be an adult whose logic tells him that he isn't stupid; if those words have been repeated often enough, he will never have the confidence to realise how much he knows or to make proper use of that knowledge.

If these words, often carelessly spoken, can have such a long-term and devastating effect, think how much good we can do by encouraging our children and praising them for what they have achieved. Whether they eventually become brilliant scholars or not doesn't really matter;

we will have played a significant part in creating a happy and confident individual – and what could be more important than that?

Stress

Stress and tension can cause temporary memory blocks. Think of the actor suffering from stage-fright who cannot remember his first line. Picture the nervous speaker on a platform about to address five hundred people and unable to think of what he wanted to say. And what about exam nerves? By the time students reach the stage of taking their final examinations, most of them know their subject pretty well. Why then do their minds go blank as soon as they turn over the question paper? The answer, of course, is stress.

If, as frequently occurs, unpleasant symptoms arise as the result of the stress – the heart races, the stomach feels as though someone has tied a knot in it – we become so aware of these sensations that we are even less able to function well. This in turn increases the sense of anxiety and the stress grows and grows.

The time to take avoiding action is before the situation even arises! You may be able to ease the tension somewhat by taking a few deep breaths but you will do even better if you are someone who regularly practises some form of relaxation. (Of course, I am assuming that you have learned your part, know what you want to say to your audience or have done your revision.)

We all know that dreadful 'it's on the tip of my tongue' feeling when a name with which we are perfectly familiar remains tantalisingly just out of reach. And the harder we try to recall it, the more elusive it seems to become. Yet some time later – when we are relaxing and thinking of something completely different – why, there it is. Now, how could we ever have forgotten it?

A certain amount of stress is good for us. The flow of adrenalin can help the mind to react quickly in a given situation. It is the *excess* stress which causes the problems. For this reason, in order to work more efficiently with your mind, it is essential to know how to calm and quieten it.

In the next chapter you will find exercises and techniques which will enable you to improve your mental agility. However, it is important to look first at how to relax your mind. These are two simple techniques which may help you. Practise each one until you are familiar with it – and, if you can resist the temptation to turn the page too quickly, do this before you go on to the next chapter.

Method 1: Sit in a comfortable chair or lie on a bed or the floor – whichever you prefer. But do make sure that your head is supported. Close your eyes and take several deep breaths. Relax your body and let your breathing become easier as you feel the tension flow out of you. Now picture in your mind something gentle and peaceful – perhaps white clouds drifting in an azure sky; perhaps gentle wavelets on a sandy shore. The idea is to find an image which pleases you and which is both tranquil and repetitive. If pleasant thoughts and memories come into your mind, look at them and enjoy them before returning to your chosen image. If unpleasant or worrying thoughts enter your head, don't try and *force* them out or you will become tense in mind and body. Acknowledge their existence and tell yourself that you will think about them later – then let them go. Continue for ten to twenty minutes.

Method 2: Choose a record or tape of a piece of music which pleases you and put it on the turntable or in the cassette player. Now sit or lie comfortably as before. As the music begins, concentrate for a few moments on relaxing your body in the usual way. Once you are relaxed, focus your attention on the music and see what images come into your mind. You may 'see' the music in shapes and colours or you may simply experience a feeling of peace or deep emotion. It is a good idea to practise this technique using the same piece of music each time and the length of one side of a cassette or record (usually about twenty minutes) is just about right for this exercise.

Once you have learned to relax your mind in this way, your mental ability will be increased. In the following chapter you will find some practical ways of helping this process still further.

6

Improving Your Mental Ability

By now you should have discovered whether you are predominantly left or right-brained, thought about developing your creativity and learned about the influences on your mind and how to quieten it. Now it is time to go on and find out how you can increase your mental efficiency. This process is not as daunting as it might sound. For the most part it consists of a series of simple techniques combined with a new way of looking at the subject.

SEEING AND OBSERVING

What do we mean when we talk about 'seeing'? You actually see far more than is registered in your conscious mind – and this is probably a good thing. Think what a clutter there would be if your mind were filled with sights which were totally irrelevant to you! The problems arise when we do not pay conscious attention to those sights which *are* important and which we would do well to notice.

However, everything you see and which has been understood is lodged safely in your subconscious and can be brought to the forefront of your mind should it be necessary to do so. In an experiment conducted some years ago, twelve people were shown a ten-minute film depicting a street scene with the usual comings and goings. The members of the audience were asked to watch the film closely as they would be asked questions about it afterwards.

When the film had finished playing, twenty questions were asked which were designed to test the observation of the people present. Although there was some variation, most people managed to answer about twelve of those questions correctly. Three members of the audience were then selected at random and, having ascertained that they had no objection, were hypnotised and, while in the hypnotic state, were asked those questions which they had formerly been unable to answer. Two of those people were then able to bring their score up to nineteen and one managed to answer all twenty questions. Everything they had seen had registered in their subconscious mind without them even being aware of it and, using hypnosis, it was possible for them to recall facts and images they did not even realise they knew.

Of course there is no way of knowing that we all see the same thing. I know what I see when I look at the grass and I have been told that the colour is called 'green'. But perhaps you do not see the same thing as I do. Perhaps, when you look at a velvet lawn you actually see the colour which I call 'red'. You will still call that colour 'green' because you too have been taught that grass is always green.

In order to see something clearly, your eyes have to be focused upon it. If that object is still, your eyes must be still. If the object is moving, then your eyes must move too. Otherwise the result will be a blur – rather like trying to take a photograph from the window of a moving vehicle. Most of us have difficulty in reading the names of stations as our train rushes past. This is because we try to move our eyes along the name, whereas the sign itself remains still. The trick is to aim your eyes at the sign as soon as it is in your line of vision and then to fix your gaze upon it as you go past. You will have about one second – which is plenty of time – in which to read the name.

When you are sleepy the muscles around your eyes relax and your vision may become blurred – remember what it is like sitting and listening to a boring speaker and how difficult it is to focus clearly upon him. The blurred effect also arises when you are under extreme stress, only then it is because the muscles become so taut and rigid that you are not able to see clearly.

Seeing and observing are two completely different things. We tend to observe what interests or concerns us and not the rest. If you walk into a room full of strangers and there is only one person in that room whom you know, you will immediately see and recognise that person, however many people are in the room, because here is something which interests you – your human oasis in a desert of unfamiliar faces.

There are several simple exercises you can do if you wish to improve your powers of observation. Here are just three of them:

Exercise 1:   Try playing the children's party game where you spend two minutes looking at an assortment of small items on a tray, then cover them with a cloth and see how many of them you can write down. Because this is a test of observation and not of memory, make sure you look at each item in relation to the others, noticing not simply the objects themselves but the pattern they form on the tray.

(A famous actor interviewed recently on the radio said that, when he had learned his part in a play, he did not just know the words he had to say but where the new paragraphs came and when he had to turn the page of the script. He was using his observation and his understanding rather than learning his role 'parrot fashion'.)

Exercise 2:   Pretend that you are a witness who is going to have to give a description to the police. Pick someone nearby whom you do not know and study their features, their build, their colouring, the clothes they are wearing and anything else you think of. Then close your eyes and see if you can describe that person in sufficient detail to distinguish him or her from anyone else – it's harder than you think but you will improve in time. This is a good exercise to practise if you are sitting in a restaurant or on a train journey – but don't let your chosen subject catch you staring or you might get a reaction you hadn't bargained for!

Exercise 3: Tip out all the pieces of a jigsaw puzzle onto the table and turn the pieces the right way up. Now select a colour – red, for example – and pick up and remove all the pieces which contain that colour. You will find after several minutes of doing this that your eye quickly focuses on the red pieces, seeming automatically to ignore all the other colours.

Total vision

You will have heard the phrase 'I could see it out of the corner of my eye'. Well, we do see a good deal of what is around us and not simply whatever it is that we happen to be staring at. If this was not so we would forever be bumping into things; it would be impossible to pass through a doorway without banging into the doorpost or to cross a room without tripping over the furniture. And yet we do not consciously look at the doorpost or the armchairs; we see them and take avoiding action automatically.

Try observing these outer images rather than simply seeing them. Stare at something immediately in front of you and make a mental note of what you can see above that object and below it, to the right and to the left. This is something you can practise at first when sitting or standing still. Later you can do the same thing when walking along or when sitting in a car (but only if you are the passenger please – don't try it while driving!)

READING

Here your eyes are given a difficult task to perform. On the one hand they must move along the lines and down the page; on the other they must be still if you are to read a word.

The difference between slow and fast readers has been closely examined. The eyes of the slow reader will stop on each word before moving on to the next one. Sometimes they will go back to look again at a word which has been passed. The eyes of the fast reader will travel along smoothly, taking in three or more words each time they stop.

The average reading speed at which comprehension is possible varies from 200–400 words per minute – with the majority of people sticking around the 200 word mark. But with a little practice you can be near the top of the scale. Pick up any book (not a children's book or one which is highly technical or full of pictures) and open it where you have two complete pages of text. Read it silently at your normal speed, timing yourself to see just how long you take. Count the number of words on those two pages and you will be able to calculate your reading speed. Make a note of your speed and the relevant page numbers. Now practise the exercises below.

1. Make it a habit to move your eyes smoothly and rapidly across the page, continuing from one line to another without a break.
2. When a child is learning to read, he will point with his finger to the word on which he is concentrating. This prevents his eyes moving forwards or backwards along the line. Try doing something similar. You might think this would slow you up but the reverse is actually true. Don't use your finger as this is too big and blocks out too much of the page; in addition the speed at which your hand moves will be too slow. You could perhaps use the tip of a pencil as a guide. This will stop your eyes wandering about the page but still allows peripheral vision so that you are able to anticipate what is coming next. Not only will you read more quickly but you will absorb more of what you read and will be better able to remember it.
3. Just as it is possible for an athlete to train himself to run faster by gradually increasing his speed, you can

do the same thing with your reading. Once you are comfortable reading at a certain pace, you can begin to move the pointer a little more quickly; your eyes will soon grow used to travelling along the lines at the new rate.

When you have practised the exercises for two or three weeks, go back to the two pages you read at the outset and time yourself as you read them again. I think you will be surprised at how much more quickly you can read while still remaining able to understand the text.

Reading and studying

If the only reading you ever do is the occasional novel or glossy magazine, then the speed at which you read probably does not matter very much to you. But, if you are one of those people who *has* to read a great deal – in connection with your job or because you are studying – then you will soon begin to appreciate the benefits of being able to read more quickly. There is no point in reading quickly, however, unless you are able at the same time to take in the meaning of what you are reading.

If you are someone who would find it helpful to be able to read and study more quickly, here are some tips to help you:

1. Before you even open the book, make sure that you are comfortable. You need a seat which supports your back and the book should be at the right distance from your eyes (the optimum reading distance is between 15 and 22 inches from your eyes). Although you should not be cold, it is better to have a room which is cool rather than too warm in order to avoid feeling sleepy.
2. You will only be able to absorb a certain amount of information at a time. If you wish to be able to learn and remember what you read, divide the material into reasonable sections before you begin.
3. Spend five or ten minutes glancing through the book.

Look at the 'Contents', the preface, the chapter headings, the illustrations, the index. This will help you to decide whether you really need to read the whole book or only certain parts of it. You will be more able to gauge what you are likely to get from *this* book, as opposed to any others you may need to study. Ten minutes spent in this way could well save you quite a lot of time in the long run.

4. If you decide that you need to read the whole of this particular book, decide how much you can cope with in one session. This will vary according to the type of book and the type of subject you are studying. A history book which may contain the facts in story form will be easier to read than one dealing with technical or scientific subjects. In the latter case it may even be a matter of reading one page in one session, whereas in the former you may be able to read and study a chapter – or even two. Don't worry if you feel you are splitting the book into very small sections. It is better to learn a small section thoroughly than to surface-read it and then have to go back to do the whole thing again.

5. Always keep a pencil and pad beside you. Make a note of any page which is of special importance and what its relevance is. Note also those facts vital for your purpose as well as anything which leads you to further research – names of other publications, for example. You don't have to write these things in great detail – in fact you would stop the learning flow if you did so; it is enough to put the page number and one or two words to remind you of the significance of what is contained there.

6. Stop every now and then; look away from the text you are reading and let your eyes focus on objects further away from you.

7. If your book has photographs, diagrams or graphs, stop for a moment when you come to them, close your eyes and try to visualise them. (More of this in the section on memory.)

WRITING

The average person writes 25 to 35 words (of five letters) per minute. With practice it is possible to increase this speed considerably, bearing in mind the following points:

1. We are talking here about notes you are taking for yourself rather than a piece of work which requires your best copper-plate style.
2. Before you begin, make sure that you are comfortable and that you feel relaxed. Does your seat support your back? Are you the right distance from your desk or table? Are your feet flat on the ground? (It is best not to twine them around the legs of the chair – or even to cross your feet or ankles – as this only causes tension on the nerve endings.) Now take a few deep breaths, have a stretch and make sure that your jaw is relaxed (no clenched teeth please) and you are ready to start.
3. If you wish to increase your writing speed, begin with sessions of two minutes or so and build up gradually.
4. Keep the pressure of pen on paper light. You will write more rapidly if you join as many letters as possible, so try using looped tails on your letters even if this is something you do not always do when writing.
5. Every now and then make sure that your writing hand is relaxed and that there is no tension in your jaw.

Note-taking

You may find yourself having to take notes at a meeting, you may be a student or engaged in research, so here are some hints to help with your note-taking technique:

Key words: Any page of text containing between 250 and 350 words probably has no more than ten key words relevant to what you need to know. The rest often consists of sentences to help convey the meaning of those key points and to make the language flow. But, once you know the key words, you are quite capable of constructing your own sentences.

As you read make a note of those key words. You may choose to circle them very lightly with a soft pencil which can easily be erased later or you may use a high-lighter pen – it rather depends on how precious the book is (and, indeed, whether it belongs to you).

Once you come to the end of the page – or some other sensible stopping point – and assuming that you have understood what you have been reading, write on your pad a heading and a list of the key words contained in the piece. Write these in capital letters rather than your normal handwriting as this will be slower and more deliberate and you are therefore more likely to remember what you have written. It is not difficult after that to learn your list of key words; you can always fill in your own sentences at a later date. If you need to write an essay about a topic, once you have written your list of key words you can use them to create a thought-flow chart.

The following passage is taken from my book 'Managing Stress' and you will see how it is possible to extract from the text the relevant key words and then to create a thought-flow chart from them:

The methods of releasing tension from the mind and body are many and various: massage, Alexander technique, hypnosis and aromatherapy are just a few which are becoming more and more readily available. Excellent as all these techniques are, perhaps the simplest and most effective form is the one which you can practise for yourself in your own home and in your own time: learning to relax.

You may be thinking to yourself that this may not be possible for you to achieve, that you are one of those people who can 'never relax'. There is no such person. Relaxation, like anything else worthwhile, can be learned. What could be more worthwhile than a simple process requiring no complicated equipment, which can not only improve the quality of your life, but could even save it?

In this chapter you will find several different relaxation techniques. Practise each one (not just once, but over a period of at least three weeks) and see which suits you the best. All it takes is fifteen minutes or so of your time twice a day – isn't it worth a try? Learn to make relaxation a habit just like cleaning your teeth. Let it become part of your daily routine. The ideal times for practising are first thing in the (morning) (yes, you *do* have the time, even if it means getting up fifteen minutes earlier), and at the (end of the day) perhaps when you arrive home from work so that you are able to 'turn off' the pressures of business and start your evening in a calm and stress-free state of mind.

Your list of key words might read thus:

RELAXATION
METHODS
SELF
LEARNED
QUALITY OF LIFE
SAVE LIFE
PRACTISE
THREE WEEKS
FIFTEEN MINUTES
TWICE A DAY
HABIT
MORNING
END OF DAY

Using that heading and the eleven listed words, you could then create the thought-flow chart on the following page. This chart could then be used as the basis for an essay or a piece of revision and – although the words used might be different – you would, in fact, end up by saying just what I said in that portion of text above. You could go one stage further and extend the thought-flow chart by incorporating your own ideas into it.

Abbreviations: If you regularly have to take notes about the same subject, you should find it quite easy to develop your own abbreviations which will make you able to take those notes even more quickly. You may choose to use initials for something which is mentioned frequently or simply to write the first half of the word. (Do be careful when using initials, however, to make sure that they can only mean one thing. Many years ago I was taking notes in a legal matter and only realised when I was transcribing them that police commissioner and police constable have the same initials. The constable might not have

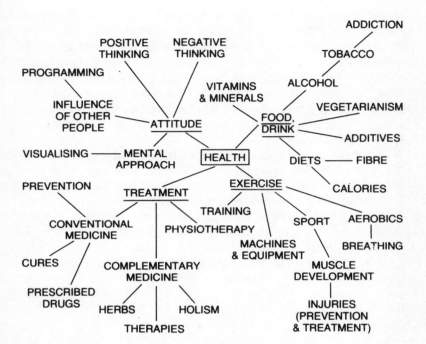

minded the instant promotion but I doubt if the commissioner would have been too happy had I relegated him to the ranks!)

NUMERACY

We all have an enormous capacity for working with figures; the only trouble is that few of us believe it. Your brain is making calculations all day long. When sitting at the breakfast table you may not actually measure the distance between your hand and the coffee cup, but you seldom miss. If you are cutting your food, you automatically calculate the size of piece which is capable of fitting into your mouth . . . and the process continues throughout the day. You know roughly how long it takes you to dress yourself; you know what time the children arrive home from school. If a motorist was not making mental calculations all day long he would be forever banging into objects, people and other vehicles. And just think of the calculations involved when a fielder runs to catch a cricket ball – he doesn't necessarily realise he is doing it but he has to work out how high the ball is, how fast it is travelling, its precise direction and how quickly he has to run in order to catch it. It makes all those dreadful school problems about taps filling baths at varying speeds seem easy!

The first thing, therefore, is to believe in yourself and in your ability to work with numbers. The rest of it can be reduced to a combination of techniques and practice. Try some of the exercises which follow; they may seem to make you slower at first, but not only will your speed increase as you get used to them, you may begin to look at problems in a different way. And remember, the aim here is not to turn you into a super-mathematician but to accustom you to thinking somewhat differently to the way you were taught at school and thereby to make things easier for yourself.

Addition: Suppose you are given a long column of figures to add. Perhaps:

$$
\begin{array}{c}
4 \\
6 \\
9 \\
2 \\
1 \\
4 \\
4 \\
6 \\
3 \\
8 \\
5 \\
1 \\
2 \\
8 \\
5 \\
3
\end{array}
$$

If you stick to the way you were taught at school, you

will probably be saying to yourself '4 + 6 = 10; + 9 = 19 . . .' and so on. Not only do most people find this tricky but you run the risk of forgetting how far down the list you have travelled. Here are two other methods of adding those same numbers:

1. Divide them into groups of the same number (pencilling them out lightly or placing a dot beside them as you do so).

Thus:

4		
6		
9		
2		
1		
4		
4		
6	Becomes:	3 × 4 = 12
3		2 × 6 = 12
8		1 × 9 = 9
5		2 × 2 = 4
1		2 × 1 = 2
2		2 × 3 = 6
8		2 × 8 = 16
5		2 × 5 = 10
3		71

The shorter column of larger numbers is much simpler to add without either making a mistake or losing your place.

2. Use the same list of numbers and arrange them in groups which add up to 10 – we all know how to multiply by ten.

4.
6.
9.
2.
1.
4.
4.
6. $4 + 6 = 10$
3. $9 + 1 = 10$
8. $2 + 8 = 10$
5. $4 + 6 = 10$
1. $5 + 5 = 10$
2. $2 + 8 = 10$
8. $4 + 3 + 3 = 10$
5.   left over = $\underline{1}$
3. $\overline{71}$

You could actually shorten this still further and, each time you make up a ten, cross it out and put I. That is,

$4 + 6 = 10$
$9 + 1 = 10$ III
$2 + 8 = 10$

and so on.

Subtraction: Working on the basis that most of us find it easier to add than to subtract, why not use addition to make the subtraction process simpler. We are taught at school that if, when subtracting, the number on the top is smaller than that on the bottom, we have to carry ten from the left, take the bottom number from that ten and then add the top one – only sometimes we find that the top number on the left is a zero which means that we have to carry ten from the one to the left of that, turn the zero into a nine and then carry the ten . . . what a complicated process. Instead of doing all that, try 'preparing' your numbers in the following way: where the top number is the smaller one, add 10 to it and add 1 to the bottom figure immediately to the left. Thus:

$$\begin{array}{r} 8392 \\ -4629 \end{array}$$

becomes

	8	13	9	12
−	5	6	3	9
	3	7	6	3

This method has the added advantage that, because it will be possible to subtract all the lower numbers without carrying anything at all, you can work it out from left to right. Since this is the way we read, it is easier and more natural to work in this way.

Multiplication: We all know how to multiply by ten — we just put a zero on the end of the original figure. And yet, if we are asked to multiply by five, we will usually go through a fairly laborious process. Since we also all know how to halve things (and are usually pretty familiar with the two times table), try this instead.

7463 × 5 is the same as $\frac{74630}{2}$ which is 37315.

Division: You can use a similar method for dividing by 50 because it is always easier to work with the number two. So simply divide by 100 (by moving the decimal point two places) and then double your answer:

974 ÷ 50 is the same as 9.74 × 2 which is 19.48

MEMORY

In this section, I am not referring to those blocks in the memory which the subconscious mind has created to prevent the subject remembering some deeply traumatic incident in his or her past. That is a whole subject on its own and one I have dealt with in another book, *Hypnosis Regression Therapy*.

What I am discussing here is the kind of recall which is part of studying, linking names to faces, remembering items on a shopping list or where you put your spectacles.

Before we go any further, try this exercise:

Think of a clock somewhere in your house. Without going to look at it, does the face of that clock bear Roman or Arabic numerals or does it have dots or other symbols to mark the numbers? Perhaps the 12, 3, 6, and 9 are the only numbers indicated. Do you know just what your clock face is like?

Now this next part is very important – READ THE NEXT SENTENCE AND THEN DO NOT READ ANY FURTHER UNTIL YOU HAVE DONE AS I ASK. Go and look at the clock you are thinking about and see whether or not you were right. STOP READING HERE!

Well, were you correct? Had you remembered the face of that clock – one which you have probably looked at time and time again? Some of you may well be surprised to find that your image of that clock face was mistaken. Before the rest of you become too smug, however, answer the next question:

What was the precise time on that clock face when you looked at it just now?

If you don't cheat, very few of you will be able to answer that question correctly. Ask yourself why this is. After all, you have been telling the time for years, haven't you? The point is, you see, that I did not ask you to go and look at the time on that clock; I merely asked you to study the numerals on it.

What is this exercise telling us? To remember something, you have to be interested in it. Very few of us forget our names, our addresses, our birthdays or the names of our children – because those things interest us. So, if you want to remember something, you must devise a way of making it interesting.

If you are to improve your memory and your recall ability, you have to learn to think differently. Learning 'parrot fashion' is adequate in the very short-term but the effects do not last for long. I can remember, before taking a Latin exam in school, sitting up half the night and learning the English 'crib' of Caesar's Gallic Wars by

heart and hoping that, when faced with a piece to translate, I would know enough Latin to work out where to
start and where to finish. I did and I passed the exam
(which seemed very important at the time, although now
I am not so sure). But two weeks later I could not have
quoted any of that translation; it had gone from my
mind, never to surface again.

Although improving your memory might seem very
much like a function of the left brain, the more you are
able to bring your right-brain skills into it, the easier you
will find it. You need to use your imagination to help
'see' pictures in your mind.

Putting names to faces: You may wish to be able to look
at someone and think instantly of his name because it
makes social life so much easier; or you may wish to
improve your chances of impressing a business acquaint-
ance (and possibly making a deal as a result). Many
people find the linking of names to faces difficult because
it is somewhat abstract – so let's take away the abstract
and instead make it interesting if ridiculous!

The trick is to use the person's name to conjure up a
picture in your mind. Sometimes, of course, it is quite
easy, particularly if the name is something like 'Rose' or
'Martin' when there really is an object with the same
name. But this doesn't happen too often, so it is usually
up to you to create your own image. And remember,
the more funny or ridiculous that image is, the simpler
it will be to remember. To show you what I mean, I
have selected a few names at random from my local
telephone directory and listed them, together with the
image which sprang to my mind (although yours might
be completely different). Here they are:

PHILLIP DIAMOND – a container full to the top (full
up = Phillip – see?) with diamonds. To make this even
more ridiculous, I decided to select the most unlikely
container I could think of, so I opted for a supermarket
plastic carrier bag. If I actually met Mr Diamond, I would
picture him clutching the bag and its contents to his
chest.

MARY SPENCER – Mary = marry, so I would see the lady as a bride coming out of a well-known High Street shop which has somehow been cut cleanly in half. (And, in case I muddled the halves and thought the lady's name was Mary Marks, I decided that it would be a very windy day and that, as the skirt of her wedding gown was blown by the gales, I was able to see that she was wearing suspenders.)

HAROLD KEEN – This one is easy! King Harold at the Battle of Hastings (no, I don't know what he looked like either – use your imagination), squinting *keenly* into the distance with an arrow sticking out of his eye.

HENRY TWIGWORTH – A gentleman with a plump hen balanced precariously on his head, standing in the market place and auctioning the twig from a tree.

I know those are daft examples – that is just why I shall be able to remember them. (By the way, in case they happen to be reading this, my apologies to Phillip, Mary, Harold and Henry for taking their names in vain!)

Finding lost items: Here your imagination can be very useful. But first of all you must eliminate the sense of panic which usually accompanies the realisation that you have lost something which is important to you. Agitation does not help matters at all. So sit down, breathe deeply and relax. Now close your eyes and allow the picture to come into your mind of where you were when you last had the item in your possession. Note that I said 'allow' it to happen; if you 'try' to remember, you will simply become tense again and all your efforts will come to nothing. If you really do not know where you were or what you were doing, begin by imagining the object itself. See it in your hand – what were you doing with it, which room were you in, in which direction were you facing? If you relax and allow the images to unfold in your imagination, in nine cases out of ten you will be able to retrace events in your mind and remember what you did with the missing object.

Remembering facts: There are two principal methods of making facts easier to remember:

1. You know those key words we were discussing earlier. Well, close your eyes and see each one being written *very slowly* – one letter at a time – inside your head. The starkness of black and white can be helpful, so let the writing be done with white chalk on a huge blackboard or with black pen on bright, white paper.
2. Think how easily we are often able to recall and describe films or television programmes we have seen. If you have to remember details about people or events, picture them in your mind (in full technicolour please) and you will find them much easier to re-create when you need to. Don't worry if you have no idea what a certain individual or a particular place actually looked like – just make it up. Does it really matter whether Marco Polo had a beard, wore an earring or had six black teeth? It is the image in your mind which is important and, as long as you are always able to link that image with Marco Polo, it will serve its purpose.

Remembering lists of items: This is where the tried and trusted Peg System comes into its own. I cannot take the credit for inventing this – it has been around for many years. But I did select my own peg words and you will have to do this too.

Take the numbers from one to ten (although of course you can continue as far as you like). As you say each one, think of a noun to rhyme with it – use the first one that comes into your head. My list goes as follows:

One   – bun
Two   – shoe
Three – tree
Four – door
Five – hive
Six   – sticks
Seven – heaven
Eight – gate
Nine – line
Ten   – hen

Once you have chosen your own peg words, they should never change. It is important that they become completely natural to you if you are to base your system upon them.

Now let us take a random list of ten items. Suppose we have:

> a vacuum cleaner
> a pink blancmange
> a sedan chair
> a dead aspidistra
> Concorde
> a word processor
> a line of washing
> an apple pie
> a Christmas tree
> a top hat

(my thanks to the somewhat bemused friend I just telephoned and asked to tell me the first ten objects that came into her mind – though I do wonder about her and what made her choose those particular objects).

Once you have your list of items, you have to link them to your own peg words. Remember, once again, to make the images as ridiculous as you possibly can. These are mine:

Vacuum cleaner (linked to one – a bun): There is nothing particularly unusual about using a vacuum cleaner to pick up the crumbs of a bun so I decided to picture a bun decorated with a vacuum cleaner on top.

Pink blancmange (linked to two – a shoe): A big black lace-up shoe filled to the brim with floppy pink blancmange;

Sedan chair (linked to three – a tree): A blossom tree with sedan chairs hanging on the branches instead of flowers;

Dead aspidistra (linked to four – a door): A heavy wooden door with a dead aspidistra instead of a handle;

Concorde (linked to five – a hive): An old-fashioned bee-hive with lots of miniature Concordes swarming out of it as the top is lifted off;

Word processor (linked to six – sticks): A word processor balanced on an untidy heap of sticks;

Line of washing (linked to seven – Heaven): A washing

line of angels' white dresses stretching from my house up to Heaven;

Apple pie (linked to eight – a gate): A huge apple pie with a gate in it – and you can imagine what you like when you get inside!

Christmas tree (linked to nine – a line): A long line starting at my feet and stretching to infinity – the line being made up of thousands of tiny Christmas trees;

Top hat (linked to ten – a hen): A big brown hen nesting happily inside an upturned top hat.

Once you have made the link, it is essential that you are able to visualise the picture it creates – it is the image you will remember not the words. After that you should have no difficulty in reeling off the list, 1 – vacuum cleaner, 2 – pink blancmange and so on. You will even be able to remember the items at random: 9 – a long line of *Christmas trees*, 4 – a *dead aspidistra* instead of a door handle . . . and so on.

Hopefully you will have found some information in this chapter which will help you with your own mental agility. But the most important thing is to learn to think in a new way – to use your right brain to assist you in dealing with subjects which may have seemed solely left-brained until now.

PART IV

The Spiritual Self

7

Awareness

To many people the word 'spiritual' has, of necessity, to be linked with religious belief – but of course this is not so. Just as it is possible to enjoy taking part in a favourite sport without either joining a club or belonging to a team, so it is possible to be a spiritual person even if you never enter a church, synagogue, mosque or any other place of religious worship.

Neither is it necessary to have what is known as a 'spiritual experience' – a single moment in time when the individual has a sense of himself and of the world in a way which transcends both the physical and the psychological. That is not to say, however, that such moments do not exist or that they do not have a profound and often life-changing effect on the person who experiences them.

Perhaps the keyword of what is meant in the context of this book by 'spiritual' is 'awareness'. Awareness of your surroundings and of yourself in relation to those surroundings. Awareness, too, that there is a purpose which exists in all situations, even if that purpose is not immediately evident.

Human life is a series of lessons and opportunities for development and evolvement and to me it seems logical to assume that one spirit continues its learning process throughout many lifetimes. I accept that there are differing views on this subject but, since no one is able to offer concrete proof one way or the other, I can only write of what I believe to be the case.

To me it seems inconceivable that a single human life on earth is the beginning and end of it all. Not only would such a concept detract from the value of human existence, I feel it would also be extremely conceited of us to think that we are all there is. I appreciate that scientists may believe our characteristics and tendencies are passed on by genetic inheritance; I accept that Jung favoured the concept of an ancestral 'memory bank' to which we are all capable of tuning in. But my own belief is that each spirit evolves by progressing through a series of different human lives, one after another, learning its lessons along the way.

My beliefs were based originally on the research and work of Dr Raymond Moody, Dr Ian Stevenson and others who have worked in the field of regression and reincarnation – not in the flamboyant, almost 'show-biz', way of some earlier regressionists but in the interests of serious study of human spiritual evolvement. These beliefs were reinforced when, as a practising hypnotherapist, I began working in the field of regression therapy in the early 1980s.

So let me lay before you my own ideas, most of which have come from the practical application of regression therapy with a wide variety of patients who came to consult me for an even wider variety of reasons. I believe that the spirit chooses which lessons it is to be faced with during the course of a particular lifetime. But, because I cannot accept the idea of total predestination, it has then to be the human being who either succeeds or fails.

Suppose, for example, a particular spirit has chosen this lifetime to learn how to deal with the temptation to do deliberate wrong to others – whether by spreading malicious lies about them, stealing from them or causing them physical harm. The individual in whom that spirit lives will be faced with the opportunity to do such wrong and it is *that individual* who makes the choice and decides which path to follow. Upon his decision (or decisions, for the opportunity may arise more than once) rests the ability of the spirit to learn that lesson and to progress to the next stage in its development.

If one accepts such a theory, then it gives a reason to all that happens to us during the course of our lives. And we are all going to have to deal with problems, great or small, at various times. How often do we ask the question 'Why me?' when faced with some personal trauma or tragedy? Perhaps it will make dealing with such a situation a little easier if we realise that there really is a reason for it and that the way in which we handle it may well go a long way towards aiding our spiritual development.

This is the holistic way of dealing with the problems with which we are all going to have to cope, whether those problems are to do with our physical, emotional or mental well-being. And we only have to look at those who are afflicted in any one of these areas to see which people seem to be evolving in spite of (or perhaps because of) their difficulties. Take physical health, for example. One person, on being informed that he has a life-threatening illness, will sit back in sad acceptance and wait for the end to come. Another who may find himself in the same situation will call upon all his inner resources in his efforts to deal with the problem. He may overcome the illness altogether but, even if this is not the case, he will certainly be able to make the most of his life and develop that special peace of mind which comes to those who are aware that they are doing all that they can to control the direction of their evolvement.

The holistic approach, therefore, calls upon us to look at a situation from all angles. If we are physically ill, is there perhaps an emotional cause for the illness? If we suffer emotionally, could there be a physical cause for our suffering of which we are unaware? If we are not able to function mentally as well as we normally do, are our minds full of anxious thoughts, emotional fears or business worries?

TAKING RESPONSIBILITY FOR YOURSELF

Becoming aware means taking responsibility for ourselves and all areas of our health and well-being. It means realising that any imbalance between our physical, emotional, mental and spiritual selves causes a loss of inner harmony and a sense of dis-ease. And it does not take much for this dis-ease of the self to become disease of the body.

To achieve the desired balance and harmony, it is essential to develop a sense of personal purpose. I am not talking here of the one-year goals and five-year goals (often money-oriented) so beloved of many modern business writers – although these too have their place. What I mean by setting goals is asking yourself 'What sort of person do I want to be?' Note that I said 'do I want to be' rather than 'would I like to be' as the latter allows for the possibility of failure. And you are not going to fail. You may trip over a couple of times on the way but you will be quite capable of picking yourself up and getting on with life until you have achieved your goal. The very fact that you are interested enough in the possibility to be reading this book makes it so.

Remember that there is no shame in failing in the short-term provided you learn from that failure and so assist your progress in the long-term. If you become aware and are willing to keep going, you cannot fail. You may not become perfect (whatever that may mean) but, if you can accept the concept of the continuity of the spirit, then you can accept that you have more than one lifetime in which to complete your evolvement.

In the next chapter you will find details of exercises in breathing, relaxation, basic meditation and visualisation – all of which are vital if you are to be healthy in a truly holistic way. In each of these a sense of awareness is essential.

Even something as purely physical as exercising brings its own awareness. We are not robots. We cannot do anything without our feelings playing a part. The problem is that most of us are so busy rushing around that we fail to become aware of those feelings and to consider what they might be telling us. Next time you indulge in physical exercise, try to become aware of your mental and emotional state during the exercise routine and after it is over.

At its highest level, sex can be a spiritual as well as a physical, mental and emotional experience. At its lowest, it can be the infliction of abuse on all these levels – and this may apply even if the sex is permitted. But at its best, sex brings about true peace with both the self and the other person – and this has nothing whatsoever to do with personal prowess, physical acrobatics or multiple orgasms. If deep love exists and that loving is complete, then this blend and harmony can be brought about by all forms of physical closeness – from touching and holding to the complete sexual act.

There is today a growing awareness of ourselves in relation to our environment. Here too holism – or balance – is vital. This is not something which can be left to governments or industry; each one of us must be aware of our own actions – what products we use, how we treat the earth and so on. Because of the differences between life in various parts of the world, we cannot escape the responsibility which accompanies the knowledge that a thoughtless or uncaring attitude in one area may seriously affect those who live in another.

It is easy for the individual to feel that his or her own small effort achieves nothing, but this is far from true. If each of us could play our own small part, those parts would link up, like the ripples on a pond, to make an earth-saving whole. There have been instances recently where vast commercial organisations and even governments have been compelled to rethink their policies and their methods because a sufficient number of individual supermarket shoppers have decided to demonstrate the strength of their feelings by boycotting a particular item.

We also have to take responsibility for how we feel about ourselves and our actions. Once we become aware of what we are doing, will we be able to go on being wasteful with our precious resources? A person who is aware of the results of his (or her) actions towards another individual will not deliberately inflict pain. And, in the same way, a person who is aware of his actions towards the world will not deliberately inflict destruction.

AWARENESS AND THE SENSES

For many people life today is such a bustling affair with so many things to get through in the day that it is not difficult to forget to be aware of what is around us. And yet this awareness does not need to take any of our precious time; it merely needs to become a part of what we are doing anyway. Try building it into your life as you use each of your five senses.

Seeing: As you walk along the street, relax in your own home or work in your office, learn to become aware of your surroundings. I know you can *see* the trees, the view from the window or the picture on the wall – but when was the last time you really *looked* at them? Notic˄ the varying colours of the trees, the grass and the sk͏ at different times of the year. Observe the expressions on the faces of people passing by. Be aware of the look in a friend's eyes – what is it telling you about him?

Hearing: After they have been in their homes for quite a short time, people who live near railway lines cease to hear the sound of the passing trains, even though the noise may seem deafening to a visitor. And most of us have forgotten how to listen to those everyday sounds which form part of our lives. The crackling of a fire, the dawn chorus of the birds, the sound of waves upon the shore; most of these go unnoticed and yet each of them can give a great deal of pleasure if we could only learn to become aware of them. Even music is so often used as a 'background noise' in shops and restaurants that it sometimes seems that we have forgotten how to listen to it.

Touching: We all know when something is so hot that it burns our fingers or so sharp that it hurts to touch it – but how much do we think about the other things we touch? Next time you open a book, stroke a cat or dog or lie between cool sheets allow yourself to become aware of the texture and the temperature of what you touch. Ask yourself how it makes you feel, what memories it arouses within you and whether you enjoy the sensation.

Smelling: It is said that the sense of smell is the most evocative of all, particularly when we are caught unawares. How often a sudden aroma can take us back to an earlier time in our lives and cause us to feel happy or sad depending on the memories aroused. Learn to become aware of the odours and aromas around you in everyday life. Some will be lovely and you will wish to savour them; others may be pretty dreadful – but at least you will know what to avoid.

Tasting: The fact that we all seem to live life in such a hurry means that much of our food and drink is taken while rushing around. That piece of toast you grab in the morning while trying to tidy the kitchen and brush your hair at the same time. The bun and cup of coffee which often replaces lunch for the busy businessman or woman. Even the evening meal – the one which used to involve being together, talking and relaxing – is often eaten from a tray on your lap while you watch television. Is it any wonder that we don't really taste our food any more? Learning to become aware of the flavour of what you eat and drink will not only give you a great deal of pleasure which you may have forgotten but it will also make you more discerning in what you choose to put into your mouth.

The journey along the spiritual path – the voyage towards awareness – is different for everyone. My journey, the joys I experience and the problems I encounter may well be totally different from those which you find yourself confronting. It is for this reason that we often feel isolated in our quest; after all, if no two people share the same experiences, no one can tell you the best way to deal with a particular situation.

Difficulties may arise because you are forced to look at the situation from two different viewpoints:

On the one hand, you need to consider yourself and be aware of yourself in all that you do and in every circumstance which arises. This takes practice but you can soon learn to use that new-found sense of awareness whether you are going through a tranquil period of your life or whether you are lying in bed wondering why you cannot get to sleep. Awareness may come easily when you are experiencing the wonder of growing a plant from seed – it is a little less in the forefront of your mind when you are standing at the kitchen sink doing the washing up.

On the other hand you need to be able to see yourself as part of a whole, to recognise the relationship between you, the world and everyone else in it. In an ideal world, if we all became truly aware of ourselves in relation to others, there would be no need for greed or violence – but we are still far from our ideal world. All you can do, if you decide to develop your spiritual self, is to do the best you can in an imperfect situation. Being aware and feeling love for mankind cannot – and should not – mean that you have to be totally submissive. You will not always be able to influence the actions and reactions of others – but then it is not your responsibility to do so. Each of us has to find our own truth and our own self in relation to the world; all you can do is to remain true to yourself and your chosen path.

Letting go

Hand in hand with an awareness of the feeling of the moment should come the ability to let that feeling go. Whether you are experiencing physical pain, mental anguish or emotional distress, you will feel it deeply at the time. When you have worked through the sensations, looked at them from all angles and asked yourself why they have entered your life and what is to be gained from them, it is important to be able to let them go. The idea is not to block them out or pretend that they never happened – indeed you would be building up a store of problems for the future if you did so – but to prevent them forming part of your future. More unhappiness and depression is caused because the person who is suffering spends too much time regretting or resenting what has happened in the past or anticipating fearfully what may occur in the future. Everything that happens in your life will naturally bring about a change in you as a person and, to that extent, your future will therefore be affected. But this is part of your journey of awareness and of the learning process your spirit chose to undertake during your present lifetime.

Forgiveness

One cannot have letting go without also having forgiveness. And this means being able to forgive yourself as well as other people. You should be able to forgive yourself once you realise that you are not expected to be perfect; indeed, if you were, you would not need to be here at all – your spirit would be continuing its learning process somewhere else. And we should all be able to forgive other people because, while we have the right to react to their words or actions in the short-term, not being perfect ourselves, we have no right to judge them in the long-term.

DEALING WITH DEATH

Isn't it strange that we are taught about many things which may never come to pass and yet most of us are not prepared for the one inevitable occurrence in our lives? No one tells us how we are supposed to deal with death – our own or that of other people – and yet we are all going to face it at some time.

It is impossible to believe in the journey of the spirit without believing that there is something else after this life. No one knows precisely what that 'something else' is – although there are a vast number of different theories and philosophies. Many people grow up frightened of what may come after this life because their minds have been filled since childhood with ideas of hell and damnation, judgment and punishment. The human mind, however, has its own limitations, being able to think only in terms of what it already knows, and there is no reason to suppose that the concept of hell and damnation is any more valid than that of angels floating on fluffy white clouds.

The death of others: There are several natural stages of human grief. These include sorrow, anger with the person who has left you, anger with the world for going on or other people for being happy, guilt for deeds undone or words unsaid and, of course, self-pity. All these feelings are normal and should not be thought to be 'wrong'. Indeed, to suppress them or even to cut them short could be the cause of many problems in the future. Once you have experienced the full range of emotions, however, you need to be able to let them go – both for your own sake and that of the one who has died who must be allowed to continue on his (or her) own spiritual journey, wherever that may take him.

Whatever your beliefs with regard to an after-life, there comes a time when you realise that you cry only for yourself, for your lonelines and the fact that you have been left behind. If you are convinced that there is nothing after this earthly life and that death is the ultimate finality, then you cannot be crying for the one who has died for he cannot now be suffering in any way at all. If you believe that there is something more after this life and that the spirit of the person who has died is continuing its journey in that place, then, because that is as it should be, there is no point in crying for that spirit. And, if you do believe in the continuation of the spirit, you have the added comfort of knowing that there is no such thing as 'never' and that people do not stop loving one another just because they are on different planes.

Your own death: If they are honest, most people are not

so much afraid of being dead as they are of the way they arrive at that state. This is understandable as, given the choice, no one wants to go through great suffering or pain. Yet it is often those who have been told of their own imminent death who are most able to come to terms with the idea. Of course they will go through all the natural stages of refusal to believe what they have been told, of anger and of unhappiness. But eventually they come to accept the situation and seem able to live each day more perfectly and more beautifully than the rest of us are able to do.

This does not mean that you should be morbid and spend each day thinking about your own death but, as you journey through this life, you will come to form your own ideas about what is to follow. Of course you will not know whether you were right until you get there – but it certainly helps if you can learn to see this lifetime as a small part of a much greater voyage.

SOME THOUGHTS WHILE SEEKING TO FULFIL THE SPIRITUAL SELF

* Whenever you experience anger, jealousy or any other destructive emotion, it is all too easy to blame other people for these feelings. And yet they, like peace and tranquillity, can only come from within you. You choose whether to hold on to bitter emotions or to let them go.
* You are an individual with a mind and a will of your own. You choose what to do with your life and how to react to the joys and sorrows you encounter on the way. You are not forced by others to behave the way you do, so do not put the blame upon them.
* Bitter thoughts and feelings about other people can harm only you. If you do nothing about those feelings, the recipient will probably be totally unaware of them; if you translate them into action, you may well be setting in motion a train of events which will cause harm and destruction, bringing as much grief to yourself as to the object of your ill-will.
* Try looking at people, objects and places as if you are

seeing them for the first time without being influenced by what you have known about them in the past. If you seek to see them with loving eyes, you will experience their beauty and be aware of their good points while making allowances for whatever may be lacking.

* Remember that you are part of a whole and that you are just as important as anyone else – but not more so.

* It is impossible to experience both fear and peace of mind at the same time. You have been given the ability to recognise your own apprehensions, to accept them and then to let them go.

* Life is not a rehearsal. The past has gone and no one can be sure of what is to come in the future. Live fully in the present – don't waste it. Take every opportunity to show and tell others how much you love them. Remember to show love to yourself too.

* There can be no progress without forgiveness. Forgive others for what they may have done to you in the past; and forgive yourself as well – you have probably learned much from your mistakes.

* Acknowledge just how much you have learned from those experiences which may have appeared difficult or unpleasant at the time. Had they never happened, you would never have become the person you are today.

* You cannot choose those thoughts which enter your mind spontaneously but you *can* choose whether or not you allow them to remain. Remember that harmful thoughts will hurt *you* and let them go as soon as you become aware of them.

* Everything that happens to you has been chosen by your spirit so there must be a reason, even if you are unable to see it at the time. There will come a day when you are able to understand.

* You are what you think, having become what you previously thought. It follows, therefore, that the way you think today will create the person you will be in the future. So you have some choice in who that person is to be.

* Fear cannot be experienced at the same time as love – whether we are talking of love of an individual, of mankind, of the world or of yourself. By choosing to feel

love, you have it in your power to change the nature of the relationships in your life.

* Just as you do not wish others to inflict their desires upon you, you must leave it to them to be free to follow their own direction in life. You can make suggestions, offer advice and give support but final decisions must be theirs. They must be allowed to fail if this is what they choose; if you love them, you will be on hand to help them up again.

* Giving of yourself should never be linked to what you might hope to gain in return. Only unconditional giving brings true peace of mind.

8

Extending the Boundaries

From the moment we are born we are surrounded by boundaries and barriers. It is only by overcoming these barriers and extending the boundaries that we are able to progress through life. And we are often far better at overcoming barriers when we are very young, seeming to lose impetus as we grow older. It does not occur to the baby as he tries to pick up a rattle or spoon that he will not succeed eventually. The small child learning to walk may fall over time and time again, yet he always picks himself up and has another go. He never stops to think that perhaps what he is attempting to do will be beyond his limitations – and so it is not.

As we grow older, however, our outlook seems to change dramatically. We become more aware of the existence of what we think of as our limitations – but in many cases these barriers exist simply because we put them there. If only we could learn from the little children and do away with the words 'I can't'.

There have been many occasions when, once the barriers are down, it is as though flood gates have opened and several people are able to do what was once thought impossible. Many years ago it was thought that no man would ever be able to run a mile in under four minutes. And no one ever did – until Roger Bannister came along and achieved the 'impossible', breaking that four-minute

mile barrier. The interesting thing is that, once it had
been proved that there was no such limitation, Bannister
only held the record for a matter of months. Suddenly
other athletes too could run a mile in less than four
minutes – and the only reason they had not done it
sooner was because they *believed* it was impossible.

The same thing happens throughout life. If we repeat
'I can't' to ourselves often enough, it becomes true. 'I
can't cook' one person will say; 'I can't speak French . . .
ride a bicycle . . . address a meeting . . .' Given that you
are of average intelligence and that you have the desire
to learn, you can do all those things – and anything else
you wish – if you will only stop putting barriers in your
own way.

I am just as guilty as everyone else. I tell myself that
'I am not mechanically-minded' – that I do not know
how to deal with the workings of my car or with anything more complicated electrically than changing a plug.
And yet, I know I am not stupid – I could learn if I
really wanted to. And that is the nub of the matter. I
have no real interest in mechanics or electricity and no
desire to learn about them. It doesn't matter that I may
go through the rest of my life unable to do magical things
with plugs, points and distributors. What does matter
is that so many people say 'I can't' about things they
want or need to do.

This chapter is concerned with breaking down barriers
and extending those self-imposed limitations. I hope to
be able to show you how you *can* achieve whatever you
want in life by using the power of your mind in addition
to practical lessons in whatever your chosen aim may
be. The lessons I leave to you. If you want to learn to
do the butterfly stroke, go to a swimming teacher; if you
want to be a doctor, a teacher, a lawyer then of course
you must study the relevant courses; if you want to drive
a car, enlist the aid of a driving instructor. That is just
common sense. What I hope you will realise by the end
of this book is that there is nothing you cannot do with
your life provided you have the wish to do it.

I suppose the first question you need to ask yourself
is 'What is it that I wish to achieve?' To do this you need

to be aware of yourself, your desires and aims and how to acquire whatever practical skills may be involved. 'That's all very well,' some of you may be saying. 'But I don't know what I want. I only know that I am not satisfied with things as they are at the moment.' My answer to this would be not to be in too much of a hurry. Take the time to think, to listen to your inner self, to use your intuition and to practise some of the exercises you will find in this chapter. If you allow yourself to be open to whatever thoughts come into your mind, ideas will present themselves to you for your consideration.

DEVELOPING YOUR INTUITION

Intuition, psychic ability, instinct – call it what you will. We all have it to a greater or lesser degree. And the more we learn to develop it, the more likely we are to make substantial progress along whatever our spiritual path may be. Like anything else worth having, intuitive ability has to be worked at if it is to be developed. But this is far easier to do than you might think – and the benefits are tremendous. The first stage is to practise one of the meditation exercises detailed below – not just once but over a period of a few weeks until it comes naturally to you.

Meditation is quite a simple process and does not have to entail wearing white robes, sitting on a mountainside and chanting for hours on end – although there is nothing at all wrong with these methods if that is what you wish to do. But for your present purpose it will be enough to spend perhaps fifteen to twenty minutes at a time freeing yourself from the mundane thoughts and problems of everyday life and allowing your mind to travel where it wishes. Even if you were to learn nothing from this process – and you will – the peace and tranquillity you will experience would make the whole exercise worthwhile.

BREATHING

Before you can learn to meditate, however, you first have to be able to relax. In order to relax, you need to know how to breathe properly. You might think that, because breathing is something you have done all your life, this cannot present a problem. But you would be surprised at the number of people who breathe inadequately and inefficiently from the upper chest rather than from the diaphragm.

This inadequate breathing can cause all sorts of problems from sensations of dizziness to actual pains in the head or chest. Taken to extremes, it is not dissimilar to the type of hyperventilation experienced by sufferers when in the midst of a panic attack. Perhaps our grandparents knew a thing or two when they told us to throw open the window first thing in the morning and take several deep breaths (but, if you are going to try this, do make sure you have some clothes on and that you don't live opposite a glue factory).

One of the reasons for the exhilaration felt by those who take regular physical exercise is that, because they are exerting themselves, they are compelled to breathe very deeply. This deep breathing, entailing an extra intake of oxygen, makes them feel fitter and full of energy, not only physically but mentally too. Many students find that, far from tiring them out, going for a run on the morning of an exam gives them the ability to think clearly and quickly.

Have you ever stopped to think about your own breathing pattern? Do you know whether you breathe deeply from the diaphragm or whether you take short shallow breaths from your upper chest area? Once again, awareness is the important word. Stop now and, without deliberately altering your breathing, become aware of its depth and rhythm. If you feel that you are not breathing in the way you should, here are a couple of exercises to help you.

Exercise 1: Lie on your back on the floor with your head

resting on a firm pillow or cushion. Bend your legs so that your knees point towards the ceiling, keeping the soles of your feet flat on the ground. Place your hands lightly across your ribcage so that your fingers just touch. Close your eyes. Now breathe slowly and evenly. As you draw in each breath your fingertips should be forced apart; if they are not, then you are not breathing from the diaphragm. You should actually feel your ribcage expanding with each breath you take. On exhaling, your fingertips should touch once more. Once you are doing it correctly, continue for at least five minutes, taking the time to be aware of precisely what it feels like.

If you are one of those people whose breathing is usually shallow, you may find yourself feeling a little dizzy when you start to get up after this exercise, so be sure to do so slowly.

Exercise 2: Make a habit of stopping at intervals during the day and thinking about the way you are breathing. Don't become obsessed with it but perhaps when you are waiting in a queue, standing on the station platform or simply sitting and watching television you could take a moment to become aware of your breathing pattern. Make sure that your jaw is relaxed and that you are breathing from your diaphragm.

RELAXATION

Being able to relax is possibly one of the most valuable achievements you can have. Apart from the fact that relaxation forms the basis for so many beneficial techniques, such as meditation and visualisation, it is also one of the initial stages of many different therapies. And in the fraught world in which we live, relaxation can help to reduce the stress and tension from which so many people suffer.

Although being able to relax may not in itself cure all ills, nevertheless it can overcome many stress-induced conditions and prevent others. Someone who is well able to relax is unlikely to find it difficult to sleep at night or to unwind after an exhausting day. He or she will be less likely to suffer from such common problems as migraine, anxiety attacks or phobias. In addition, it has been proved that the ability to relax deeply for as little as ten or fifteen minutes each day can go a long way towards preventing such life-threatening illnesses as strokes and heart attacks.

Being able to relax has nothing at all to do with how busy a life you lead. In fact, someone who is bored because he finds himself with too much time on his hands is quite likely to discover that his discontent and tension makes relaxation difficult. The busy businessman (or woman) may feel that his hectic lifestyle does not allow time for such luxuries as relaxation – but, when all it needs to take is ten minutes or so a day, that cannot be true. Indeed, I would have thought it well worth while getting up ten minutes earlier or going to bed ten minutes later if, by doing so, you might actually be improving your health – not merely preventing its breakdown.

What about those people who think they *cannot* relax? All I would say to them is that – like anything else worthwhile – relaxation can be learned. Here are two exercises you can practise to improve your own powers of relaxation (assuming you have already ascertained that you are breathing correctly).

Exercise 1:   Sit in a chair or lie on a bed or couch. If you are sitting upright, make sure that your head and neck are supported. Close your eyes and breathe easily and regularly.

It is easier to relax your muscles if you first of all tense them as hard as you can. So, start with your feet; tense the muscles and then let them relax. Now do the same thing with your leg and thigh muscles. Gradually work all the way up your body, tensing and relaxing one set of muscles at a time. Pay particular attention to the area around your shoulders, head and neck as this is where one usually finds the greatest amount of accumulated tension.

Once your body is relaxed and your breathing regular,

imagine that, with each intake of breath, you are being lifted gently from your bed or chair and that, as you exhale, you are being lowered gently down again. Continue for about ten minutes, then open your eyes and sit quietly for a few moments; don't just leap to your feet and rush around straight away.

Exercise 2: Start in precisely the same way as Exercise 1. When you feel that your body is relaxed, use your imagination to make each part of your body feel heavy. Once again, start with your feet and work upwards. Imagine that your feet have been turned to lead or stone and then, using the power of your own mind, *make* this heaviness spread slowly up your legs, past your knees, up your thighs to your hips. Continue in the same way with your hands and your arms, then the whole of the trunk of your body. Finally, use your imagination to make your head – and even your eyelids – heavy.

Try each of the above exercises for a week or two so that you can see which you prefer. After that, if you continue to find ten or fifteen minutes a day in which to relax, you will be doing yourself a great deal of good.

MEDITATION

Let us assume that you have now practised both breathing and relaxing techniques until they come completely naturally to you. Now you are ready to go on to learn about basic meditation.

People choose to learn meditation for many different reasons. For some it is a stepping-stone to psychic development; to others it is a means of problem-solving; yet others simply believe that is a wonderful way of finding an oasis of peace in a frenetic world. Whatever your reasons, the techniques are the same.

One of the misconceptions about meditation is that, in order to master it, it is necessary to be able to make your mind 'blank' – empty it of all thought. There are, of course, advanced meditation techniques which do incorporate this emptying of the mind but they involve a measure of dedication and devotion for which most of us do not have the time – or indeed the inclination. The aim of this book is to help you to live holistically by establishing a four-point balance in your life using simple methods which do not demand too much of you or take up too much of your time. For this reason, I prefer to suggest that you proceed gently by using a guided visualisation (see the exercises below) tc help you in your meditation, rather than find yourself growing frustrated because you cannot achieve the 'blankness of mind' demanded by some techniques.

When practising meditation exercises, it is preferable to sit rather than lie – but do make certain that you are comfortable and that your back and neck are well supported. The room should be warm but not too hot and your clothing should be comfortable. Do what you can to ensure that you will not be disturbed: ask the family to leave you alone for ten or fifteen minutes; unplug the telephone if you are on your own; do not answer the doorbell if it rings. None of these things would do you any harm but they might nullify your attempts to meditate.

Exercise 1: Begin by relaxing completely, using your chosen method. Ensure that your breathing is slow and regular. Now picture in your mind the following scene:

You are walking through a beautiful garden on a lovely, sunny day. The garden is large, with a path which twists and turns so that there is always something new to see. Eventually you see that the path leads to an old gate set in a red brick wall. The gate has a large iron handle. In your imagination, place your hands on the handle and turn it, pulling the gate open as you do so. Go through and continue your walk. What you see beyond that gate in the wall is up to you – but it is vital that you do not plan it or force any particular image into your mind. Just allow your imaginary walk to take place and the scene will unfold itself to you. Continue for as long as you wish and then, when you are ready, slowly bring your mind back to your own room and open your eyes.

If you are not in the habit of using your imagination in this way, you may find this exercise difficult at first. But don't allow yourself to grow impatient or frustrated. Simply stop what you are doing, enjoy the feeling of relaxation – and try again the next day. It definitely grows easier with practice.

By the way, there is no 'correct' image. The scene will be different for everyone and may well vary for each person from day to day. You may find it interesting to think about the pictures which came spontaneously into your mind – but please do this afterwards; do not try to question them as they appear.

Exercise 2: This technique involves the use of a silent chant. Sit in your chair, close your eyes and relax by your chosen method. Making sure that you breathe correctly from your diaphragm, silently say to yourself the sound 'ah' each time you inhale and 'um' as you exhale. Don't say the sounds aloud or move your lips – all the chanting is done inside your head.

You may find that this is all you do for the full period of your meditation. But it is not at all uncommon for those practising to begin to see shapes and colours – or even images – in their minds as they continue this silent chant.

Exercise 3: Begin in the usual way. Once you are completely relaxed and breathing evenly, continue with the following image:

You are lying on soft, green grass in the shade of a huge, old tree. Although as you meditate your eyes are closed and will remain so, in your imagination your eyes are open. As you look above you, you can see, hanging from a long silver thread attached to the tree, a beautiful crystal. The sun shining through the branches of your tree catch the angles of the crystal sending rays of different coloured light darting from it. Concentrate on the crystal, focusing all your attention upon it, until you become unaware of the tree, the sunlight or the silver thread – the crystal needs to fill your whole mind. As you stare at your crystal, different thoughts or pictures will come unbidden into your mind.

When you feel that you have finished the exercise and have brought yourself back again to your own room, it is a good idea to make a note of anything you have seen or felt during the course of this particular meditation. This is a technique which often leads to the development of psychic or intuitive ability and, although the images may seem to have little relevance today, it is possible that they will come to mean something to you in the future. You will not remember them, even though you think you will, so do write them down.

DEVELOPING PSYCHIC ABILITY

If you wish to develop your own psychic ability – and remember we all have this potential within us should we wish to make use of it – there are certain rules you *must* remember.

1. In the course of psychic work, one receives information from somewhere else. Now, it does not matter if you want to think this information comes from God, from your Spirit, from your guides, from your higher self – or anywhere else. The fact is that we need to open up in order to be able to receive it. If you are going to allow yourself to be open in this way, it is essential that you seek protection before you begin. After all, you would not go out for the day leaving your front door ajar, would you? You might be very lucky and a kind neighbour could come and shut it for you – or you might have the misfortune to return and find that vandals have ransacked your home. In the same way – particularly when you are inexperienced – it is necessary to ensure that you do not receive psychic information which would either hurt or distress you. For this reason, you need to be protected – and this will be achieved simply by you asking that it be so.

2. Detailed below you will find a method of opening up the chakras so that you are in the best possible condition to receive the information given to you. It is essential

that, once the session is over, you remember to close down the chakras again so that you do not become vulnerable.

3. Psychics receive their information in many different ways – and none of them is right or wrong. Some people see images clearly in their minds; others hear words spoken to them; others will simply find that they 'know' something without being aware of how that knowledge arrived. When you first start working to develop your own psychic ability, any information you receive may well be somewhat haphazard in nature. Please don't worry about this – things will sorts themselves out in time. In the meantime, keep a pen and paper handy and make a note of anything you do receive. It could well be that something which seems meaningless or trivial today could be extremely significant in the future.

THE CHAKRAS

'Chakra' is actually a Sanskrit word meaning 'wheel' and chakras are often depicted in diagrams as wheels or discs. In fact the chakras are the centres of energy in the human body. There are seven main chakras and these are:

1. The Crown Chakra (at the centre of the top of the head)
2. The Brow Chakra – also known as the Third Eye Chakra (at the central point between the eyebrows)
3. The Throat Chakra (at the centre of the base of the throat)
4. The Heart Chakra (at the centre of the chest area – not over the heart itself)
5. The Solar Plexus Chakra (a few inches above the navel)
6. The Spleen Chakra (just below the level of the navel)
7. The Base Chakra (about six inches below the navel)

In order to be aware psychically it is necessary to open up these chakras in the following way:

Starting with the base chakra and working upwards,

focus your attention on the area of each one in turn and then find a way of opening that chakra. Some people like to imagine the area becoming warm, some to see it suffused with light, while others visualise a flower (often a rose or a lotus) unfolding in the appropriate area of the body. You must use the image you feel is most appropriate.

Progress upwards through each chakra, concentrating particularly on the brow and crown chakras. Remain in that 'open' state for as long as you wish, being aware of any information you might receive.

When you wish to bring the session to an end, simply reverse the process by reducing the heat, letting the light fade or the flower close – this time making sure that you start with the crown chakra and work down to end with the base chakra.

Once the session is over, do remember to give thanks for any information you have been given. Even if you do not feel you learned anything in particular, you can still offer thanks for the sense of peace and tranquillity you will have experienced.

HEALING

We have already discussed healing in the sense that, by taking care of yourself physically, mentally and emotionally, you will be doing the very best you can to maintain your health holistically. However, there also exists the ability to heal oneself or others spiritually.

The most common concept of spiritual healing is the laying on of hands but there are also other methods. After all, what is healing but the giving of love, whether by touch or the power of thought? The parent who comforts a small child by 'kissing him better' is practising the most natural form of healing there is.

True spiritual healers are by nature humble for they accept that the healing power does not originate from them but from a higher energy force (whether known as God, Spirit or by any other name). The healer himself is simply the transmitter; the means of passing that healing energy on to the one who is in need of it.

There are organisations who will help you should you wish to train as a spiritual healer but you can also learn the basics for yourself. And the meditation which is so invaluable for those who wish to develop psychically is also a necessary first step for any would-be healers.

Of course there are many who scoff at the idea of spiritual healing having any effectiveness whatsoever. These doubters claim that any benefit felt results solely from the belief of the patient. To such sceptics, I would say two things:

1. If you are right – does it really matter? If someone is helped to feel better by whatever means, who cares whether healing really exists or whether they are using the power of their own mind?
2. How do you tell an animal what to think? It is not uncommon for healers (and also homoeopaths and acupuncturists) to work on sick animals. When these animals get better, is it because they have believed they will? I think not, as I do not yet know of anyone who has been able to communicate on such a level with dogs, cats, horses or any other animal.

No ethical healer will tell you to give up any form of medical treatment you may be receiving. Healing works effectively when used side by side with either orthodox or complementary medicine. Of course, there are some people who choose to use only healing and natural therapies – but that is a highly personal decision and the only person who can reach it is the patient concerned.

Suppose you would like to learn how to give healing – what do you do? Firstly you need to practise a meditation technique until you are comfortable with it. Then follow the stages listed below:

1. Before beginning a session, relax deeply for several minutes and ask that you be given the ability to help the person concerned. Remember also to ask for protection for yourself so that you are not vulnerable to any negative energies which may surround that

person. At the end of the session of relaxation, use your mind to visualise your hands absorbing pure spiritual energy – you may find that your hands become quite warm as you do this.

2. Let's suppose that your 'patient' has a pain in his upper back. There are two basic ways of working on this. You can either place your hands directly on the area of his body which is painful and then, closing your eyes, ask for that healing power to be directed through your hands to his body (you may wish to visualise this power in the form of a shaft of white light). If you prefer not to touch the person concerned, you can heal his aura. The aura is an energy force surrounding the body and, when there is something wrong with the body, the aura itself is damaged. Place your hands over the painful area but about four to six inches away from the body itself and, once again, ask for and visualise the healing energy. Whichever method you use, your patient should begin to feel heat in the afflicted area.

3. At the end of the session, which need take no more than five or ten minutes at a time, sit quietly and give thanks for having been allowed to help a fellow human being.

4. Because very few people are cured of anything in a single session, it may be necessary to repeat this process several times at regular intervals.

5. It is not advisable to try to heal another person if you are feeling unwell yourself – or even if you are going through a tense or anxious time in your own life – as you could transmit this negativity to someone who is already vulnerable.

Self-healing

When healing yourself, laying on of hands is obviously not really possible so you have to rely on a combination of relaxation and the power of your own mind. You can bring about dramatic improvements in a wide variety of conditions by using visualisation or positive imagery.

There are two aspects to positive imagery:

1. You can 'see' in your imagination the afflicted area looking well and healthy again. This is particularly effective when dealing with an actual wound; if you can visualise it as having healed, the natural healing process is likely to take place far more quickly than it would otherwise do.
2. Use your powers of creative visualisation to see the healing take place symbolically. Let me give you a couple of hypothetical examples to explain precisely what I mean.

* You suffer from migraine and have already established that this is due to tension rather than because of an allergy to a particular food or drink. Of course, by learning to relax, you can reduce a great deal of the tension and thereby make the migraine attacks less frequent. But that doesn't help you with the pain you are feeling in your head right now. So, sit or lie comfortably and relax as much as the pain will allow. Now, visualise a piece of ice resting in the very centre of your forehead. Because your head is warm, that piece of ice is slowly melting and the cool water is spreading over the whole of your forehead and down behind your eyes, easing away any pain or throbbing which might be there. Continue this exercise for several minutes or until the pain has receded.
* You have a stomach ulcer which gives you frequent sharp pain. Having relaxed in the usual way, visualise the whole stomach area being bathed in a cool, white liquid which soothes the inflammation and nullifies the pain.

From the simple examples given above, you will see that it is possible to create a suitable image for any condition you may have. But please remember that those examples assume that the cause of the pain has been discovered. If you suffer regular pain of any sort, it is vital that you have a check-up or examination so that the reason for it can be found. Constant or repeated pain is there as a warning, to tell you that something is wrong, and should not be ignored. Remember too that using this method of self-healing is not intended to take the place of any other treatment you may be receiving.

POSITIVE IMAGERY

You have seen how positive imagery can help you when dealing with your physical health. But it can also be of benefit in many other ways. If you are nervous and lacking in confidence, or if you are anxious (whether continuously or because of a specific event), you can learn to harness the power of your mind to help you deal with the situation.

Suppose you are uneasy about a specific occasion in the near future, what can you do? That occasion may be an examination, a job interview, meeting a new group of people, making a speech . . . the possibilities are limitless. But you can use positive imagery to help you, whatever it may be.

Let's take one example. You have been asked to make a short speech at a forthcoming meeting and, as the day grows nearer, you find yourself becoming more and more nervous. Here's what you do:

(I am assuming that you know what you want to say and have prepared the speech itself – no amount of visualisation can replace the groundwork.) Start this routine about two weeks before the date of the speech: every day set aside ten or fifteen minutes when you know you can be alone and undisturbed. Begin by relaxing as you have already learned. Now picture in your mind the scene on the great day – but make sure that you visualise everything turning out just as you would wish it to. See as much detail as possible. If you know what the place where you will make your speech looks like, so much the better. Imagine the whole scene almost as if you were watching a play or a film. See yourself standing on the platform, notes in hand, making the speech like a true expert. You will not be flushed or shaking but calm and collected. Imagine, too, the approval and interest on the faces of your audience as you hold their attention.

While you are imagining all this, keep reminding yourself that you are completely relaxed. In this way, your subconscious mind will form a link between the image in your mind and the feeling of relaxation which will come to the fore when the occasion actually arises.

All you are doing here is rehearsing the scene in your mind, just as you would rehearse your part in a theatre production. And, because practice makes perfect – even if that practice is only in your mind – you will give a perfect performance when the time comes.

That is one simple example but I assure you that you can use precisely the same technique to deal with any one-off situation as well as any ongoing anxieties you may have.

CONCLUSION

You now have all the ingredients to make the perfect cake, you have watered your seeds so that your garden may be full of beautiful flowers and the petrol tank of your car is full.

I hope this book has helped you to see that the harmony and balance intrinsic in holistic living can help you to live a richer, healthier and more fulfilled life than you may previously have thought possible – and that it is not really so very difficult to achieve that balance.

So enjoy the cake, have a garden full of flowers and take a long drive – live as well and happily as it is possible for you to do.

Further Information

FURTHER READING

Bremness, L. *World of Herbs*, Ebury Press, 1990
Buzan, T. *Make the Most of your Mind*, Pan Books, 1981
Markham, U. *Elements of Visualisation*, Element Books, 1989
Norfolk, D. *Fit for Life*, Hamlyn, 1980
Roet, B. *All in the Mind*, Optima, 1987
Taylor, J. *The Shape of Minds to Come*, Michael Joseph, 1971

CASSETTES FOR SELF-HELP AND RELAXATION

Available from:

Thorsons Publishing Group Ltd.
78–85 Fulham Palace Road
London W6 8JB

The Hypnothink Foundation
PO Box 154
Cheltenham
Glos. GL53 9EG

USEFUL ADDRESSES
(a sae in each case would be appreciated)

Bach Flower Remedies
Mount Vernon
Sotwell
Wallingford
Oxon OX10 0PZ
(details of Bach Flower Remedies and training courses)

British Holistic Medical Association
179 Gloucester Place
London NW1 6DX
(information on holistic and complementary medicine)

British Society for Nutritional Medicine
5 Somerhill Road
Hove
E. Sussex BN3 1RP
(names of nutritionists)

The Hypnothink Foundation
PO Box 154
Cheltenham
Glos. GL53 9EG
(books, cassettes and courses in various forms of self-help)

Index